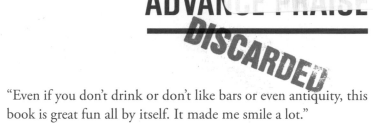

"Even if you don't drink or don't like bars or even antiquity, this book is great fun all by itself. It made me smile a lot."

—Mark Medoff, Tony Award–winning playwright of *Children of a Lesser God*

"And I thought I'd been to a lot of bars! *Bucket List Bars* showed me just how many bars I still have to make it to—looks like I'm going to have to scratch the Grand Canyon off the list and, instead, head to Denver to hit El Chapultepec, Tucson for the Kon Tiki, and the dozens of other hidden gems Dr. Clint Lanier and Derek Hembree have uncovered. This book will inspire readers to get out and see the bars that built the country (not to mention the tiki movement). Finally, a guidebook for people like me — I'll never travel to an American city without it again."

—Christine Sismondo, author of *America Walks into a Bar: A Spirited History of Taverns and Saloons, Speakeasies and Grog Shops*

"I think this can become a great guide for both travelers and locals alike. A way to discover and rediscover our nation's history. I've always said, 'There's no better place to get an education than in a bar.' Well, this is a listing of some of the best learning institutes in America. Most are practically museums as well. The walls and the tenders tell a fascinating story. Best of all, you can virtually visit by watching the online videos that are linked via QR codes. These guys must've had a blast creating this incredible work. Cheers!"

—Sother Teague (a.k.a. @CreativeDrunk), head bartender at Amor y Amargo in NYC's East Village

"Travelers need gems in every city like the ones that Clint Lanier and Derek Hembree describe in *Bucket List Bars*. Readers will gain a descriptive road map and insight into the most historic and iconic bars in America, while also learning about some of the nearby attractions to see—or not see—after knocking back a few."

—Louie Ryan, owner of the Townhouse Saloon and Del Monte Speakeasy

"*Bucket List Bars* is a clever project that highlights the unique watering holes of America. The authors exhaustively researched the most interesting and oldest taverns and inns in the country that are maintaining their history. The book is a great guide for travelers or anyone who wants to learn a little while they imbibe in the nation's great traditions. It's concise, interesting and will make any reader thirsty!"

—Chef Walter Staib of City Tavern Restaurant, Emmy Award–winning host of *A Taste of History*

"*Bucket List Bars* is a must-read for any booze enthusiast who loves history and BOOZE! The commitment to this project shows that there is more to drinking than just drinking but rather a deeper understanding of the social significance that bars have in our culture. Each bar has its own personality with walls whispering of its tales. Gun and knife fights, prostitution, gambling, bootlegging, and good ol' fashioned imbibing are some of the stories you can expect in this book. I will be sure to stock this book behind my bar at the Brooklynite to add to the growing list of must-have bar books."

—Jeret Pena, master barman and owner of the Brooklynite, StarChefs.com Rising Star Award winner, and James Beard Foundation nominee

BUCKET LIST BARS™

HISTORIC SALOONS, PUBS, AND DIVES OF AMERICA

DR. CLINT LANIER & DEREK HEMBREE

EMERALD
BOOK CO.

Published by Emerald Book Company
Austin, TX
www.emeraldbookcompany.com

Distributed by Emerald Book Company

For ordering information or special discounts for bulk purchases, please contact Emerald Book Company at PO Box 91869, Austin, TX 78709, 512.891.6100.

Design by Martin Riggenbach

Publisher's Cataloging-In-Publication Data
(Prepared by The Donohue Group, Inc.)

Lanier, Clint.
  Bucket list bars / Clint Lanier & Derek Hembree.—1st ed.

    p. : ill. ; cm.

  ISBN: 978-1-937110-43-7

  1. Bars (Drinking establishments)—United States—Guidebooks. 2. Bars (Drinking establishments)—United States—History. I. Hembree, Derek. II. Title.

TX950.56 .L36 2013
647.9573   2012954447

Part of the Tree Neutral® program, which offsets the number of trees consumed in the production and printing of this book by taking proactive steps, such as planting trees in direct proportion to the number of trees used: www.treeneutral.com

TreeNeutral

Printed in the United States of America on acid-free paper

13 14 15 16 17   10 9 8 7 6 5 4 3 2 1

First Edition

CONTENTS

PUB CRAWLS
FOR THE TRAVELER

I t's time to come clean about bars and traveling. The combination typically just doesn't work. Most of the time you're stuck in the hotel even after getting through with the business of the day. In a new city you might wander down to the lounge on the ground floor to see what's available.

You scan the crowd and see a pretty homogenous group of people just like yourself. Eventually you resign yourself to stay there and take a seat at the bar to watch some random sports or news channel with the sound turned down, eating below average but way-overpriced food, and facing a three-tap beer selection.

No more. This book is for the traveler who wants to find the interesting, hidden and out-of-the-way locales to unwind in after a day of meetings or classes.

Or, this book is simply for the traveler that appreciates the institutions that really built this country.

In each location, Bucket List Bars™ brings you the most famous, infamous or historic and culturally significant watering holes you can find. These are the places you'll be talking about for weeks after you visit. Have fun. Be safe.

SO WHAT'S A BUCKET LIST BAR™?

We're often asked what a Bucket List Bar™ really is. Unfortunately, the explanation isn't that simple. Perhaps the most basic definition is to say that these are the places around the country and around the world you want to have a drink in before you die.

But Bucket List Bars™ are more than just watering holes. They're not places you go to just drink. They're places you go to experience. These are places that have a history. Sometimes it's good, sometimes it's bad, but it's always worthy of time and investigation.

Bucket List Bars™ have character. No two are alike and all are original. They define their own style and include décor and atmosphere often imitated but never, ever duplicated.

These aren't chain places. They might be owned by a corporation, and they might not be the only one in a portfolio of bars, but they're not places exploited, copied and then shared with the world in cut-rate versions across the continent.

Bucket List Bars™ have no defining look. Some are elegant while some, frankly, smell like last week's stale beer. Some serve cocktails that take ten minutes to make while others serve one kind of beer and nothing else.

They could have mismatched furniture or priceless artwork, gleaming brass or faded wood, crystal and porcelain, or red Solo cups.

But all of these differences—every single one—are what makes these Bucket List Bars™.

If they were people they wouldn't be Brad Pitts or Kim

Kardashians, they'd be James Browns and Jack Kerouacs. They'd be people who made their own way—people who didn't try to fit in—but simply did what they did until the world took notice and then put them on their deserving pedestals.

Bucket List Bars™ are innocent in that they didn't set out to be Bucket List Bars™. They simply set out to provide the basic necessities—companionship, food, drink and entertainment—to society. At some point the world took notice and now *we're* putting them on their deserved pedestal.

WHY DO WE SELECT THE BARS WE SELECT?

Let's be honest; there are a lot of bars out there. Many are good and worth a stop-in for a drink. However, we're confident that the bars we present are the best to visit in any given area.

We can be that confident because of the research we put into finding them. We first start with the source. We tap our social media networks and then ask for recommendations. We scour the internet and look at reviews, read the history and local accounts, newspaper articles, biographies and visitor records.

But let's be even more honest; anyone can do that stuff. Many books and articles do—they rely on secondary sources for their information and recommendations.

We take it a step further and visit. Proof of this are the documentaries we make of every single one of the places we include.

We interview the owners, the bartenders, the customers and then give you that history in the videos. If they have a signature drink, we ask them to make it so you can see whether or not it's worth trying (they usually are).

And it's at this stage we determine if a place is a Bucket List Bar™ or not. This is the point when we figure out really quickly if this place is worthy of your visit or not. If not—if it turns out that even after our research, our visit, and interviews we determine the bar to be a loser—we don't bother telling you about it. There are a handful of bars we didn't include in this book just for that reason.

But those we do include are vetted and tried and definitely worthy of you. These places have a great history, a notorious past, and sometimes a dubious present.

WHAT ABOUT THE BUCKET LIST BARS™ IN THIS VOLUME?

This book presents the Bucket List Bars™ from 12 regions around the United States. The focus is on the historic bars from these regions.

Historic in the truest sense has nothing to do with age—though we did track down the oldest two bars in the nation. When something is historic it is significant to the culture and society around it at the time and into the future.

There have been thousands of bars and saloons in the United States from its founding until now. Only a handful survived, but they are not all equally historic. True, they're all old and significant in terms of architecture or simply in their atmosphere, but not all saw a gunfight. Not all were used to imprison a famous

British spy during the Revolutionary War. Not all have become the quintessential dive bar or Old West Saloon.

In short, not every old bar is historic.

And in fact, not all of the bars in this book are really that old. We present bars from the 1960s and 1950s. Does that make them less historic?

When you read about them, and definitely when you visit them, you'll understand.

The value of these places is in what they present to the people who decide to have a drink in them. They reflect the history of a region, of a people, of an event or of a way of life that's now long gone. Or, as in the case of the most recent bar—Mother's Nightclub opened in 1968—they represent the start of something. In Mother's case it's the start of whole movements in music and everything that was inspired by those movements.

And this list isn't complete. Here we present 40 of the most historic and worth-your-time watering holes from only 12 places around the country. There are many more we still need to discover and bring to you, and that will happen soon.

Until then, use this book to find the hidden treasures in the cities you probably already visit quite frequently. Go have a drink (or a few) in these places, and let them know you found out about them in this book.

HOW TO USE THIS BOOK

This book is divided into 12 major regions in the United States. We try to give you not only the Bucket List Bars™ from these regions, but also other notable bars to try. These bars didn't make it into this book simply because they lacked that extra something to make it on your bucket list, but they're in the area and if you have the time you should still check them out.

At the end of each bar we review we also provide some nearby distractions that you really should visit if you're in the area. Many of the distractions have some kind of connection to the bar itself, so it's worth your while to see them.

We also provide the name and phone number of local taxi and ride companies. Please use these if you decide to make the trip into a pub crawl. Some of the bars we review are near enough that walking might be possible, but often they're on different sides of a region. Please don't drink and then drive.

Lastly we include QR codes for each destination. The QR codes when scanned with a smart phone will take you directly to our YouTube-hosted documentary about the bar (below each QR code is the direct link address for those without smart phones). The documentaries help to put each bar in context, show you what they look like inside and out, and provide a much more in-depth and colorful history of the bars than a simple guide could do.

For those bars that have some type of signature drink, we've also included QR codes that link to videos of the bartenders mixing these drinks. These are the drinks we tried and loved when we were there, and are our recommendation for trying when you visit.

http://youtu.be/BIW47KJLi-Q

THE BARS OF BUCKET LIST BARS™

I n this book we're covering 40 of the most historic bars in the United States spread over 12 different regions—from New England to San Francisco with plenty of stops in between. Not all bars are created equal, however: they are all different, not only in their personalities but also in their types. There are at least five different bar types we'll talk about over and over: Taverns/Pubs, Saloons, Speakeasies, Dives, and Tiki Bars. Here we'll try to define them in their historical context.

TAVERN/PUB

In our modern vernacular the terms, "Tavern" and "Pub" have come to mean the same things. But it wasn't always the case.

Pubs, or public houses, and taverns can trace their history all the way back to the Roman Empire. During the Empire's four-century control of Britain it created a vast and extensive network of roads throughout Britain and Europe. Along these roads were alehouses, taverns, and inns that offered travelers a place to stop for a drink, food, supplies, or a place to sleep.

Alehouses of the time were usually ordinary dwellings where the householder would serve home-brewed ale or beer, and if lodging was offered it was commonly a simple spot on the floor or a loft in a barn. A tavern on the other hand typically served only wine, and since wine was more expensive at the time taverns catered to the upper class. Another major difference was that taverns were limited to towns whereas alehouses could be opened in just about any dwelling where the occupant wanted to sell their home brew and possibly offer travelers a place to stay.

After the Roman Empire collapsed and during the 18th century the term alehouse was gradually replaced by the term public house, as alehouses were growing in size and grandeur. In 1810 we see the first purpose-built public houses erected in London, England and quickly expanding to towns across the country and eventually the world. These establishments were usually the focal point of a community and there was a time in some countries (like Holland, for example) when towns would not officially be recognized as such unless they had a pub and/or a tavern. The pub had become a place where the common public could grab a meal or a drink, talk of local, national and world news, do business and often times find some form of entertainment.

Similar to public houses taverns began to evolve after the collapse of the Roman Empire. In 18th century England we see many of them actually transformed into coffee houses catering to the wealthy while others turned into extravagant inns, and still others remained taverns. In the Colonial US they were an important part of the community and were often supervised by county officials. These establishments were eventually licensed to house guests, turning them into inns, and were the earliest forms of what we know today as hotels. They were an essential part of life for travelers who relied on them for shelter for themselves and their horses, and as a place to find food and entertainment. Plus, they acted as a town's post office and most importantly, a place to enjoy an alcoholic beverage.

Today for the most part a pub and a tavern are the same, though very different from a lounge, a dive bar, club, or Tiki bar. They usually have significant European influence in their décor, building, food menu and in their founding history. Their drink menu can vary vastly with beer and whiskey almost always the cornerstone of the bar. Though they were founded during the rule of the Roman Empire they still survive today as the foundation for almost any drinking establishment or hotel you find yourself in.

SALOONS

Saloons are about as American as apple pie.

When you think of a saloon the first thing that probably pops into your head is a character like Josey Wales walking into an old dusty bar with swinging doors, a piano player pelting out an old tune, gambling off to the side, ladies of the night advertising their wares and an old barman cleaning a glass behind the bar. In all truthfulness only some of what we called saloons would have been quite so extravagant.

One of the earliest saloons opened in Brown's Hole, Wyoming, in 1822 to serve fur trappers and traders. Geographically close to Wyoming's border with Utah and Colorado, this establishment was the first of thousands of similar places to be dubbed saloons during America's expansion west. Shortly after the first saloon opened its doors more started popping up just about anywhere and everywhere.

Built out of tents, wagons, sod houses, ship hulls, cut into the side of hills, built from the ground up, shady and extravagant, they were built in almost every small town, city or cross roads that dotted the western frontier. But no matter how, where or what they were constructed of they all served the same purpose: a place for cowboys and soldiers to spend their off hours, where a lonesome traveler could find conversation or companionship, and even where a businessman could strike a deal.

Though there were many different types and differing levels of luxury in the various saloons of the country, the alcohols they served were often limited. Beer was not uncommon, but without pasteurization and refrigeration its quality would have been questionable at best. Some places served Cactus Tea or Cactus Wine, which was made from a mixture of peyote and tequila (we wonder what kind of buzz that brought on). But at the forefront of alcohol served in saloons was whiskey. Oftentimes made from raw alcohol, burnt sugar, and chewing tobacco, it was called numerous names like Tarantula Juice, Red Eye, and Coffin Varnish. Most places also served house rotgut that was often 100 proof and cut with turpentine, ammonia, gunpowder or some kind of spice, like cayenne.

Legend has it that if an unknown or foreign patron entered a saloon and ordered a strange or "fruity" cocktail, or if he was to stand around and only sip his drink, bar patrons would sometimes take it upon themselves to force the stranger to drink a fifth of rotgut for his own good.

Saloons today are for the most part a thing of the past. Most places that still call themselves saloons are either still open or reopened from the days of the old west, like the Crystal Palace in Tombstone, or are opened in the spirit of the traditional saloon, like Broken Spoke in Sturgis, South Dakota, and in Daytona, Florida. Regardless of when they were built, a saloon today is used in much the same manner as a saloon of yesterday. They exist for the common good of the public as places to find a conversation, blow off some steam, catch a game, meet some new friends, grab a bite to eat, or simply spend some time contemplating the meaning of life.

SPEAKEASY

Many believe that speakeasies came about during the notorious period known as Prohibition. And while that is when these establishments were in their heyday, they actually came into existence long before the 1920 start of Prohibition.

The term speakeasy refers to an establishment that illegally sells alcoholic beverages. There are many legends as to how the term came about but one of the most commonly told is the story of Kate Hester. Kate owned a bar in Pittsburgh, Pennsylvania which she operated as a legal establishment until 1888 when the state of Pennsylvania raised the price of bar licenses from $50 to $500 dollars. Kate refused to pay a 1000% increase and instead took her bar underground. She would tell her patrons to "speakeasy boys" when they became too loud so as not to attract the attention of law enforcement officials.

The term has become synonymous with establishments that sold alcohol during the United States' experiment with Prohibition from 1920-33. From notorious gangsters like Al Capone to the everyday working man and woman, speakeasies served as a reprieve from the oppression of the Noble Experiment. They most commonly served hard alcohol, especially gin due to its ease of distillation, and beer was an uncommon luxury. When Prohibition was repealed with the 21st Amendment, often these very same establishments turned into legal neighborhood bars or returned to being the bars they were before the onset of Prohibition.

When we refer to speakeasies in this book we are referring to places like The Green Mill in Chicago and The Townhouse in Venice Beach, California that were actually speakeasies during Prohibition. Places like these are still in operation today and still retain that original ambiance. Walking into them will often give you the feeling of being transported to another time period. You'd almost expect Al Capone to walk in any minute and sit down with you for a drink or two.

DIVE BARS

A dive bar is one of the original American bars: a staple of Americana if you will.

The history of how the dive bar came about is steeped in

mystery. Some believe the term was used to describe illegal drinking establishments similar to speakeasies, which were mainly located in basements (thus you had to "dive" under the street or building to get in). Others believe the term came about because it was in these seedy establishments that patrons would "dive" under their tables and chairs to get away from gun fights and/or bar brawls—a sometime necessary evil of being a patron of an exceptionally seedy dive bar. Further adding to the mystery is the fact that no one knows which bar was the first 'official' dive bar, and saloons or even speakeasies could also be labeled dives on their journeys through history.

One of the most notorious is the saloon/speakeasy turned dive called King Eddy's Saloon in L.A. King Eddy's is located beneath of the 120-year-old King Edward hotel and was once the hub of L.A.'s notorious bootlegging operation made possible by a gigantic network of tunnels running under the city. During Prohibition the bar was located in the basement and was a favorite among local cops.

When Prohibition ended King Eddy's moved back upstairs amongst L.A.'s rapidly declining Skid Row. Today the old-timers and youngsters mix and mingle in a diverse crowd, and the place opens at 6am which just so happens to be the same time Happy Hour blessedly starts. In the end this place was a legend among dive bars the world over until it was recently bought out by a local corporation with plans for renovations, leaving a huge question mark as to what kind of establishment will exist upon reopening.

Most places don't start off as dive bars (though some places try to) and they aren't created from a corporation's drive to take advantage of a trend. A dive bar is a reputation and an atmosphere that has to be earned and developed over the course of years. It's a badge that is worn with honor; a place that welcomes all (most of the time) and is known for the great times you typically can't remember, cheap drinks and regulars who become like a family. If your chief mission is to forgo the craft cocktail or regional beer (most Dives specialize in cheap American beers and equally cheap shots of whiskey) and instead eliminate sobriety, then a dive is the place for you.

Today's dive bars are usually dark, run-down, with odors of questionable origin, ever-present beer signs and sports flags, and Christmas lights haphazardly hung on the walls and fixtures. Regardless of their dubious characteristics dive bars hold a special place in almost any bar patron's heart. It's in these places you feel no different than the movie star sitting on your right or the bum on the left. There's no special section, no VIP area, the prices are easy on almost any pocketbook and the food is almost always a bad idea. And while all of these characteristics may be the very reason you would avoid some bars, they're also reasons you come to a dive bar.

Regardless of how the term came about there's one thing that's certain: dive bars are one of America's greatest gifts to the world.

TIKI BARS

The 1950s and 60s found the United States in a state of change, self-discovery, and newfound world prominence on the heels of World War II. The middle class was taking the country by storm with ever-expanding lifestyles that included the suburbs, 2.4 kids, a two-car garage, and a shift in the American dream. Concurrently consuming the nation were Tiki bars and Tiki culture, which eventually led to at least one Tiki bar in almost every US city.

It all started in 1934 when Ernest Raymond opened his Polynesian-themed bar and restaurant in Hollywood, California, called Donn the Beachcomber. Ernest, who later changed his name to Donn Beach, found inspiration for his new establishment from his time spent sailing throughout the South Pacific. He opened the bar and restaurant in the hopes of bringing a piece of Polynesian "Aloha" to the people of Southern California through a unique atmosphere, tropical drinks, and a Polynesian-themed menu. Little did he know that he had started a whole new American subculture that would both grow to epic proportions and survive the test of time.

Today Tiki bars still sweep their patrons away to an island oasis. Known for their tropical drinks with recipes guarded more tenaciously than the gold at Fort Knox, unique décor, and a one-of-a-kind atmosphere, these places are a unique gem amongst the community of bars. They have an ever loyal following that are known to literally travel the world in search of the perfect mai tai and perfect Tiki oasis. You could be in the middle of a bustling city, but when you step into the confines of one of the great American Tiki bars you will find a Polynesian oasis awaiting your arrival.

NEW YORK CITY AREA

No city in the United States boasts more history—as it concerns alcohol and drinking—than New York. The very first brewery in the new world was founded here in 1612 by a couple of Dutch immigrants named Adrian Block and Hans Christiansen. Its first distillery, probably making hard apple cider (called applejack), was founded in 1640 on Staten Island. The first US gin distillery—Anchor Gin—was built here in the early 19th century.

Even things we take for granted today started out related to New York's booze industry. Take paved streets for example. The very first paved street in America was the street in New York City that fronted the many breweries. *Brouwer Street,* now known as Stone Street in the Financial District, was paved in 1658 to keep the wagons, heavy with kegs of beer from the breweries, from sinking in the mud.

Then there are the drinking places. New York City, filled with immigrants since its founding, has seen an immense number of bars, alehouses, porterhouses and grog shops. In fact, one of the most booze-soaked areas in the nation in the late 19th century was New York City's own Bowery. In this area the city's street gangs clashed and controlled gambling and prostitution. Flophouses and cheap booze were everywhere, and the value of a man's life was less than the cost of a quart of rum.

As for bars, this is one of the best destinations in the country for historic and truly unique places. The saloons in this area are some of the oldest in the nation, and a decent Bucket List Bar™ pub crawl could be made here.

TRANSPORTATION: Taxis are plentiful in New York City, and are readily hailed at any of the bars here except for Old '76 House. All bars except Old '76 House and Bridge Café are close to subway stations (Bridge Café is close to a bus stop that can be taken to the closest station). Old '76 House can be reached on Coach USA buses (depart from GW Bridge beginning at 7:10 and 7:40am and every hour at 10 and 40 past until 10:40pm: trip is approximately 30 minutes). Tappan is small enough to easily walk to the tavern from drop off.

McSORLEY'S OLD ALE HOUSE

NEW YORK, NY

15 East 7th Street
New York, NY 10003
(212) 474-9148
http://www.mcsorleysnewyork.com/
http://youtu.be/t6ThJe3Foyc

Food: Yes
Live Music: No
Hours: Monday—Saturday 11am–1am, Sunday 1pm–1am
Type of Bar: Pub
What to Drink: McSorley's Ale
Why You Should Go: Sheer history, artifacts lining the walls, little changed in 150 years.

The year was 1854 and "The Bowery" in lower Manhattan was a place only the poorest degenerates would frequent. You couldn't fall down in this neighborhood without falling into a tavern, a bar, or a pub. It was here that John McSorley, an Irish immigrant, opened one of the most historic taverns in the US, "The Old House At Home."

THE HISTORY

The history of McSorley's is a bit confounding. If you talk to the bartenders and read their website you'll learn that John McSorley (the founder) was born in 1827, arrived in the US in 1851 (making him 23 years of age upon arrival) and opened his bar in 1854.

But contradicting this is a New York Times article taking issue with McSorley's claims. According the article McSorley didn't appear in city directories until 1862. Also, the article claims the building the bar occupies was built no earlier than 1858. And finally, a census taker who visited McSorley in 1880 recorded 1855 as the year McSorley arrived in the US.

Whatever the case may be, we'll go with what we were told. McSorley's was founded by Irish immigrant John McSorley, who was born in Tyrone, Ireland, in 1827. In 1845, when John was approximately 18 years old, the Irish Potato Famine began, eventually killing one million and displacing a million more who emigrated to the US.

John arrived in the US in 1851 and three years later opened a tavern called "The Old House at Home." Like many taverns at the time it was a gentleman-only space, which eventually led to a motto they became famous for: "Good Ale, Raw Onions, and No Ladies."

In 1875 John apprenticed his son Bill McSorley in the running of the bar. Bill took over the bar in 1905 only to be fired by his father after he began selling liquor. Up to that point they had only sold the ale John himself created and brewed in the basement.

When Prohibition began in 1920, McSorley's survived by serving Near Beer, created during Prohibition with an alcohol level below .5%.

In 1936 Bill McSorley sold the bar to Daniel O'Connell, a patron and NYC policeman, who was the first non-McSorley to own the bar. Bill passed away in 1938, shortly followed by O'Connell in 1939, who left the bar to his daughter, Dorothy. Dorothy had made a promise to her father to not change or manage the bar, much to the patrons' relief, and her husband, Harry Kirwan, stepped in and managed the bar until his death.

In 1964 while visiting Ireland Harry Kirwan's car broke down, and he was picked up by a Good Samaritan by the name of Matthew Maher. Harry told Matthew that if he ever decided to come to America and was in need of work, to come by the bar. Matthew took him up on the offer shortly after their meeting in Ireland and worked as a bartender, waiter, and manager at McSorley's until 1977, when he bought the place from Harry Kirwan's son, Danny. Mathew still owns the bar today and chances are you'll find him sitting in the back enjoying a sandwich and laughing it up with his employees.

McSorleys is known for its motto, "Good Ale, Raw Onions, and No Ladies." Yes, it serves great beer (its own recipe still, but now made offsite), yes, it serves raw onions with practically everything, and yes, for well over 100 years they didn't allow women. In fact, the men-only policy was such a part of the bar that not even the female owner in 1954 would go in during normal business hours (only on Sundays when the bar was closed).

That all changed when on January 9th, 1969, two women, Karen DeCrow and Faith Seidenberg, attorneys and members of the National Organization for Women ("NOW") entered the bar, seated themselves, had multiple requests for service denied, and were finally escorted out by the bartender.

According to DeCrow, a man at the bar initially bought them a round when their requests were ignored. She stated that while the patrons did not turn on them, they did in fact turn on the gentleman who offered to buy them the beer. She claims he was forced out bodily with his face covered in blood.

The case against McSorley's went all the way to federal court, and in 1970 DeCrow and Seidenberg won. Shortly afterwards the New York mayor signed a bill barring discrimination in public places, which would have ended McSorley's men-only policy anyway.

McSorley's did seriously consider becoming a private club but decided against it, and on August 10th, 1970, the bar officially opened to women. Rumor has it that then-owner Danny Kirwan wanted his mother to be the first woman served, but she refused saying she would not break the promise made to her father.

TODAY

Today McSorley's is one of the most well-known historic bars in New York City. It's a great example of the Irish-owned saloons that peppered the Bowery in the 1800s and has a charm and class reserved for those very respectable but aged examples of what's not made any more, like a '57 Chevy, or maybe Robert DeNiro.

The crowd is composed of business professionals at lunch or after work, along with locals and a college crowd making the rounds. Interject these groups with a steady stream of never-ending tourists from across the globe, and you have a lively and rambunctious atmosphere.

The bartenders are no-nonsense and put on a show of glib toughness, but they are all heart (one guy who hadn't been in for over a year stopped in while we were there, and the bartender asked how his daughter was—she had been sick the last time the guy was in).

Take the time to slowly walk around and view all of the artifacts hanging on the walls. You'll see the original newspaper announcing Lincoln's assassination, JFK's death certificate and countless other priceless objects that should be in a museum (and arguably are).

Take a moment to study the gas lamp immediately in front of the bar. Hanging from the light fixture you'll notice a bunch of old and dusty wishbones. Legend has it that McSorley would give an ale and turkey dinner to soldiers preparing to head off to war. As they headed out the door, they'd hang the wishbone on the lamp in hopes of returning. If the soldier did return he would remove the wishbone. Those hanging are from soldiers who never returned. In a way, these bones are their memorial.

THE FOOD

The food at McSorley's is not only reasonably priced, especially for New York City, but it's also delicious. Especially try their two traditional sandwiches, liverwurst and corned beef. The corned beef is moist and tender, and the liverwurst has just the right amount of spice. Served on Jewish rye with thick slices of liverwurst and thin slices of raw onion, it's tasty, filling, and the perfect start to an evening of ale. Be sure to try their spicy house

Dijon mustard. We recommend you spoon some onto almost anything, as it has great flavor and a nice spicy kick.

THE DRINKS

McSorley's has stayed true to John's wishes and serves only ale, light and dark. The original recipe was created and brewed by John McSorley himself, but as demand for it increased he sold the recipe to a brewery called Fidelio. From there the brewery itself and recipe changed hands numerous times. Breweries such as Rheingold, Schmidt's, and Stroh brewed McSorley's Cream Stock Ale and Lager until it finally found a home at Pabst Brewing Company.

NEARBY DISTRACTIONS

Empire State Building

www.esbnyc.com

350 Fifth Avenue New York, NY 10118 (212) 736-3100
(Monday-Sunday 8am-2am, the last elevator up is at 115 am).

Once the tallest building in the world, and still one of the most recognizable, the Empire State building is as New York as Apple Pie is American. This is the perfect stop on your way to or from McSorley's, about a mile and a half away, and we highly recommend going up to watch the sunset and the city lights come on. Pay the extra money to get the VIP pass (otherwise you could easily stand in line for an hour or more) and enjoy the breathtaking views from this iconic skyscraper.

Artichoke Basille's Pizza

www.artichokepizza.com

328 East 14th St. New York, NY 10012 (212) 228-2004
(Monday-Sunday 10am-5am).

If you're in the mood for some outstanding NY pizza then look no further than Artichoke Basille's Pizza. Only about a half mile from McSorley's, and open until 5am, they're famous for their artichoke pizza, which has been described as "more addictive than crack." Be forewarned, it's popular, so there's probably going to be a wait.

Katz's Delicatessen

www.katzsdelicatessen.com

205 East Houston Street New York, NY 10002 (212) 254-2246 (Monday-Wednesday 8am-10:45pm, Thursday 8am-2:45am, Friday-Sunday 8am-10:45 pm).

Less than a mile from McSorley's sits the fabled Katz's Delicatessen. Opened in 1888 and featured in movies like "When Harry Met Sally" ('I'll have what she's having…' fake orgasm scene) and in the cult classic, Donnie Brasco, this place is as legendary as NY pizza. The food is outstanding and the pastrami and corned beef sandwiches are made to epic proportions.

SAM FRAUNCES TAVERN

NEW YORK, NY

54 Pearl Street
New York, NY 10004
(212) 968-1776
http://www.frauncestavernmuseum.org
http://youtu.be/3bP2YxPTigc

Food: Yes
Live Music: Yes
Hours: (Museum) Monday—Sunday 12pm-5pm, (bar)
Monday—Sunday 11am-4am
Type of Bar: Tavern
What to Drink: Craft beer or an Irish whiskey
Why You Should Go: One of the oldest bars in America,
where George Washington partied when the British left
New York.

This place was *the* bar in its day. The building dates back to 1719, and it was here that George Washington gave his farewell address to his officers of the Continental Army in 1783. It also housed the offices of the Department of War, Treasury, and Foreign Affairs and took a direct cannonball hit from the British Navy at the beginning of the Revolutionary War. To sum it up, this was our Founding Fathers' watering hole before and after we earned our independence.

THE HISTORY

The building was originally built as a residence for the Delancey family, one of the wealthiest families in New York at the time (though the family never actually lived here). The building was eventually sold to a tavern keeper by the name of Samuel Fraunces in 1762. Fraunces set about immediately turning the building into the immensely popular "Queen's Head Tavern."

In colonial America, the local tavern was a place that commoners went to read newspapers (if they could read), listen to newspapers being read aloud, get reports of local goings-on, retrieve their mail, and, of course, to have a meal and enjoy a drink or two. Jennifer Patton, Fraunces Tavern Museum Education Director, summed it up nicely to us when she described them to be like today's message board found at almost every Starbucks across the country.

Fraunces founded the "Queen's Head Tavern" during the very turbulent times leading up to the American Revolution. At the time New York City found itself divided into two groups—the

Loyalist and the Patriots—and most taverns reflected the cultural divide.

Fraunces was a Patriot bar. One could even say that Fraunces' was the Patriot tavern headquarters, as none other than George Washington and John Adams frequented the establishment and discussed, debated, and some even say plotted the beginning of the Revolutionary War.

Though it is unclear as to what occurred in the tavern during the time the English occupied the city, Fraunces Tavern played a significant role in the celebrations that occurred on November 25th, 1783, also known as "Evacuation Day." Evacuation Day was the day the British soldiers left New York for good, signaling the end of the war. And it was on this day George Washington paraded back into New York City and headed straight to Fraunces Tavern where a grand celebration was held. During the celebration George Washington himself, armed with hot-buttered rum, made 13 toasts to everyone from the American Army to the Kings of Sweden and France.

TODAY

Today the tavern is more museum than tavern, with the top floors serving as a museum and the bottom floor currently leased out to the Porter House Company, which operates a colonial-themed restaurant and bar. It is also considerably larger, with renovations that include three surrounding buildings.

The Queen's Head Tavern ceased to exist over 200 years ago,

but what stands today is a reminder of what we are, where we came from and who we became. If you find yourself in New York and have the time to visit, then stop by Fraunces Tavern, spend some time thoroughly going through the museum, paying particular attention to the Long Room (which is where Washington gave most of his speeches and toasts) and the artifacts that let you get a glimpse of life during the formative years of our country.

Don't forget, this is the place where George Washington and John Adams would have discussed the revolution, what we would be as a country, and schemed and planned against England. It's also the place Washington himself came to celebrate after winning the war. You could say this is where the revolution started and ended.

After your museum visit take a few minutes to absorb everything while enjoying a cold one in the bar on the bottom floor (it is also called Fraunces Tavern). They offer a full menu of traditional Irish faire that would be perfect for a crisp autumn day or cold winter night.

They also feature a huge beer selection, both on tap and in bottles. Right beyond the front entrance is also a whiskey bar, for tasting and sampling many of the exclusive Irish whiskies they carry.

THE FOOD

The food selection at the Porter House Restaurant features upper-end classic pub grub, especially of the Irish kind. Expect fish and chips, shepherd's pie, and many of the other usual menu items.

However, they do feature great cuts of meat for their steaks, and from what we've heard, great pastas.

THE DRINKS

They have an extensive Irish whiskey collection, many from tiny distilleries you'd never find in a typical liquor store here in the states. Their whiskey tasting room is pretty overwhelming, but they're patient and spot-on with recommendations.

They also have a huge assortment of taps flowing with craft

beers from here and abroad. It would seem fitting to get a Guinness but don't: go with something you can't get anywhere else.

NEARBY DISTRACTIONS

World Trade Center Memorial

www.911memorial.org

1 Liberty Plz #20 New York, NY 10006 (212) 312-8800 (during ongoing construction a timed reservation system is in place—reservations can be made online and we recommend you plan well in advance).

A memorial to honor the nearly 3,000 innocent victims of the infamous 9/11 attacks, few places in the world are more hallowed than this location. Only a mile from Fraunces, this should be a required stop as part of your historical journey.

Statue of Liberty

www.statuecruises.com

Liberty Island, New York (open every day except Christmas though hours change by season).

To the world she's both a beacon and a symbol of freedom and democracy. Lady Liberty is one of America's most iconic land marks. To get to Liberty Island you will need to take one of Statue Cruises ferries, the only company that has access to the island. They leave from Battery Park, which is less than a half mile from Fraunces.

Ellis Island

www.statuecruises.com

Ellis Island, New York (Open every day except Christmas, though hours change by season).

Today it's a museum, but at one time it was the gateway to America for millions of immigrants. As a matter of fact about half of the current US population can trace their lineage back to an ancestor who passed through Ellis Island. If you plan on going to the Statue of Liberty, Ellis Island is a short ferry ride away and included with the same ticket.

BRIDGE CAFÉ
NEW YORK, NY

279 Water Street
New York, NY 10038
(212) 227-3344
http://www.bridgecafenyc.com
http://youtu.be/-wChZOtxe0A

Food: Yes
Live Music: No
Hours: Monday, Sunday 11:45am-10pm,
Tuesday—Thursday 11:45am-11pm, Friday 11:45am-
12am, Saturday 5pm-12am
Type of Bar: Pub
What to Drink: Old Fashioned
Why You Should Go: Oldest continuously serving bar in
New York City, great cocktails and food, colorful history.

Located at 279 Water Street in the shadow of the Brooklyn Bridge, Bridge Café has been serving the public in one form or another since it was built in 1794. It began its current run of continuously serving or selling alcohol when Newell Narme opened a grocery and wine and porter bottler, which makes it the oldest alcohol-serving establishment in New York City.

THE HISTORY

The history of Bridge Café is more the history of the building than it is the Café itself, according to manager Adam Weprin.

The structure was built in 1794 and has served as a saloon, restaurant, porterhouse, grocery, brothel and smugglers' den. Above all, it has been an establishment that served alcohol off and on from 1794 until 1847, at which time it began its current run of continuously serving alcohol (both legally and illegally), making it older (because it has continuously served alcohol) and younger (since it has had multiple bars and owners) than McSorley's or Pete's Tavern.

The seaport area in which the building resides was a nest of mariners, pirates, and criminals, and just about every building in the district was either a brothel or grog shop.

In 1847 Henry Williams rented the building and created the porterhouse that marked the beginning of the 155-year run of serving alcohol.

Perhaps its most notorious period was from 1859-1881, when it was run as a saloon by a Thomas Norton. A period article from the New York Times reported a police raid on the area

brothels, and stated that "twenty two of the most repulsive types of degraded women stood huddled together at the prisoners bar in the Tombs police court yesterday and the women were taken out of the following buildings 275, 277, 277 ½, and **279 Water Street.**"

The upper floors of this building had multiple brothels from the 1850s until the establishment was indicted in April of 1879 as a "disorderly house."

The building saw multiple saloons from then until Prohibition, when, as a restaurant, it sold "cider" supplied by Brooklyn bootlegger Charlie Brennan.

TODAY

The building was bought by the current owners in 1979. They renamed it Bridge Café and set about restoring the many floors of the building—which is, as they say, an ongoing project.

Early clientele of the building would probably never

recognize it if they were to wander inside: the white tablecloths and gleaming bar (with a 150-year-old lead-glass mirror), speak to the elegance the current owners have instilled in the place. What they have created, from a former grog-shop and brothel, is an upscale café serving gourmet seasonal cuisine, fine cocktails, beer, wine and spirits.

Speaking of spirits, Bridge Café has a few of its own. As is common with many of the establishments we've visited, Bridge Café is rumored to be haunted. From footsteps on the second floor, stereos that turn themselves up and down, smells of lavender, computers that constantly break, ghosts that like to drink and leave their mess behind, and whispered answers to questions asked by the living, Bridge Café does seem to have a thing or two going on in the paranormal category. Ask manager Adam about it when you visit.

THE FOOD

They describe the food at Bridge Café as high-end comfort food, but that may have been a slightly inadequate description. Perhaps a better description is "a tasty, unique, and ever-changing menu with something for everyone, served by an outstanding wait staff, and created by friendly and brilliant chef Joseph Kunst."

We were lucky enough to try a variety of dishes that included deep fried pork bellies, fried oysters, buffalo steak, duck, diver scallops, key lime pie, and pumpkin flan. The food and service are outstanding.

THE DRINKS

Bridge Café has a full service bar that includes over 85 single malts from all over the world, as well as dozens of bourbons and rye whiskies.

But if you are lucky enough to visit when Adam is working, ask to have him make you an Old Fashioned. First documented in Hudson, New York, in 1806, an Old Fashioned is bourbon, Angostura bitters, sugar and muddled cherry and orange. It is said to be the first cocktail ever mixed, and Bridge Café mixes them perfectly. So perfectly in fact we have no reservations when we say that the Old Fashioned at Bridge Café is the best Old Fashioned we have ever tried.

http://youtu.be/TDhwqEtRirw

NEARBY DISTRACTIONS

Brooklyn Bridge

Since you're going to be right next to it, why not walk the Brooklyn Bridge? Starting at City Hall Park, less than a half mile away from Bridge Café, there is a dedicated pedestrian walkway that runs above the bustling car traffic. Depending on the weather the views can be outstanding, and it is an easy return trip back by either walking, hopping on the subway, or during the summer months, taking the New York Water Taxi.

Grimaldi's Pizzeria

www.grimaldis.com

Under the Brooklyn Bridge, 1 Front St. Brooklyn, NY 11201 (718) 858-4300 (Monday-Thursday 11:30am-10:45pm, Friday 11:30am-11:45pm, Saturday 12pm-11:45pm, Sunday 12pm-10:45pm).

If you decided to walk across the Brooklyn Bridge why not treat yourself to some well-deserved pizza, and what better place than Grimaldi's? Sitting in the shadow of the bridge, this epic pizzeria features a hand-built coal-fired oven. Constantly voted best pizza in Zagat, it's well worth the walk, or ride, to get a slice or two.

Wall Street

Wall Street New York, NY (always open, though most businesses, like the New York Stock Exchange, have hours posted on their website).

You can't think of stocks, trading, commodities or just about anything financial without thinking of Wall Street. Less than a mile from Bridge Café, this financial hub either hosts or has hosted several of the world's largest exchanges, including the NASDAQ, New York Mercantile Exchange and the New York Stock Exchange. Unfortunately, few places offer tours anymore (they probably don't want you to see what they are doing with your money), but it's worth a visit to see one of the most storied locations of the financial world.

OLD TOWN BAR
NEW YORK, NY

45 East 18th Street
New York, NY 10003
(212) 529-6732
http://www.oldtownbar.com
http://youtu.be/0UpDJo-4uow

Food: Yes
Live Music: No
Hours: Monday—Friday 11:30am-1am,
Saturday 12pm-2am, Sunday 12pm-12am
Type of Bar: Pub
What to Drink: A martini or other classic cocktail
Why You Should Go: Immaculate bar, conversation, urinals.

Listed as one of Esquire's Best Bars in America for 2010; a Frank McCourt hangout; used in a number of films, shows, commercials, music videos, and late night comedy shows (The Devil's Own, Mad About You, Sex and the City and the opening scene of The David Letterman Show, to name just a few); and featuring urinals that are over 100 years old, Old Town Bar is described as "New York as it was and as it is."

THE HISTORY

Sitting on East 18th Street in New York City and widely considered a writer's bar, Old Town Bar originally opened as a popular German establishment called Viemeisters in 1892. During Prohibition the bar renamed itself Craig's Restaurant, became a speakeasy and was supported, frequented, and protected by members of the nearby Tammany Hall.

Tammany Hall was a Democratic Party political machine that is rumored to have used its power to control and manipulate New York City and State politics while helping immigrants, mainly Irish, rise in the American political system from the 1790s to as late as the 1960s. So while Tammany Hall supported Craig's Restaurant, it had little to worry about.

During Prohibition, Old Town Bar (Craig's Restaurant) took advantage of a special feature built into its booths, a feature still present today. The top of each booth can be opened to reveal a convenient hiding spot. The booths and their hiding places got their 15 minutes of fame when they were featured in the film "Izzy & Moe," which was directed by Jackie Cooper, starred Jackie Gleason and Art Carney and focused on the era of Prohibition.

After Prohibition ended, the bar reopened as the Old Town Bar and was owned and operated by the German-American Loden family. At the time the neighborhood consisted mainly of German immigrants and their families, and as such, it specialized in German food. The Loden family owned it until the 1960s when Larry Meagher took over the day-to-day operations. Larry had unsuccessfully tried his hand at bar ownership in Brooklyn before finding himself running Old Town Bar. He eventually purchased the bar at a time when the surrounding area and New York City were awakening from their 1960s economic and cultural slump. Luckily for Larry and his family, he seemed to have found his calling at this place.

TODAY

Featuring an impressive 55-foot mahogany bar; some of the oldest, still operating dumbwaiters in New York; dozens of photos of visiting actors, writers, and politicians; giant urinals, and 16-foot pressed tin ceilings, walking into Old Town Bar is almost like walking into vintage New York. The place is quiet, low-key class with clientele ranging from tourists to college students, to local businessmen, writers and actors.

We asked current owner and operator Gerard Meagher to describe The Old Town bar today and feel he summed it up nicely when he said, "*We* celebrate writers, and *this place* celebrates conversation."

Frequented by writers like Frank McCourt, Irish playwright

Brian Friel, Irish poet Seamus Heaney, and English novelist Nick Hornby (plus no loud music, no blaring TVs, and a no cell phone policy), it is easy to see why writers and normal everyday people are drawn to Old Town Bar.

This is one of the few remaining bars (another being My Brother's Bar in Denver) that is truly conducive for conversation between friends and strangers over drinks. It's a setting that unfortunately is quickly disappearing from today's pubs, where the ever constant cell phones, televisions, laptops, and iPods flood the atmosphere and douse any hope for quiet discussions.

The bar is a throwback to the way things were before all of the interruptions of digital gadgetry, to a time when people came to the bar to socialize with each other. And so today the bar is as it was, which makes it unique.

And speaking of unique, one of the most unique features of Old Town Bar is the ancient set of urinals found in the men's bathroom. Originally installed in 1910, the urinals have become almost as celebrated—and maybe even more so—than the bar itself. In fact, they are so celebrated that on November

1st, 2010, the bar celebrated the urinals' 100th birthday with champagne and a congratulatory letter from Mayor Bloomberg (which is still posted at the entrance to the restroom).

THE FOOD

The food is classic Irish/New York cuisine, including soups and sandwiches, pastas and salads. They are known for their hamburgers, so you'd do well to try one with a cold beer or nice red wine.

The seating area for the restaurant is located upstairs, as is the kitchen. If you order in the bar downstairs you'll have your food delivered by one of the last remaining, original dumbwaiters still used in the city.

THE DRINKS

Old Town Bar features a full service bar and a long list of beers on tap. You won't find much in the way of trendy drinks here, so plan on sticking to the classics, which they do well. A martini, a Manhattan or any other traditional cocktail should be the drink of choice when here.

NEARBY DISTRACTIONS

Theodore Roosevelt Birthplace
www.nps.gov/thrb
28 East 20th Street New York, NY 10003
(Tuesday-Saturday 9am-5pm).

Theodore Roosevelt is, to date, the only US President born in New York City, and this is your opportunity to visit the area of his childhood home. Located less than a quarter of a mile from Old Town Bar, Teddy spent the first 14 years of his life in this very location. He would later become an author, explorer, Governor of New York, Nobel Peace Prize recipient, Colonel of the Rough Riders and President of the United States. Though the house is a rebuilt replica (the original was demolished in 1916), it contains many of the original furnishings provided by Roosevelt's sisters and wife.

Broadway
www.broadway.com
(showtimes and theatre locations vary; visit website for schedule and tickets).

A short distance—about 1.4 miles—from Old Town Bar is the start of the legendary Broadway Theatre District. With a long list of shows running year-round, numerous theatres to choose from, and some of the best live performances on earth, it has something for everyone. Check out their website and book early, as some of the more popular shows are sold out far in advance.

Times Square
www.timessquarenyc.org
Times Square New York, NY.

Few people think of New York or New Year's Eve without thinking of Times Square. Simply a major commercial intersection at the junction of Broadway and Seventh, Times Square has become one of the most visited tourist attractions in the world. A leisurely mile and a half from Old Town Bar, be sure to visit this electronically charged epicenter of New York City.

 # EAR INN
NEW YORK, NY

326 Spring Street
New York, NY 10013
(212) 226-9060
http://www.earinn.com
http://youtu.be/y4bqniYw-Qc

Food: Yes
Live Music: Yes
Hours: Monday—Sunday 12pm-4am
Type of Bar: Pub
What to Drink: Shot of Jameson and a Guinness
Why You Should Go: One of the oldest bars in the United States, serving continuously since 1833, brothel and grog shop for the waterfront

Originally built in 1817 as a home for James Brown, a man whose racial identity to this day is still contested, and named the Ear Inn in 1977 to avoid a lengthy review by the Landmark Commission, this lower Manhattan bar is a not-to-be-missed spot for enjoying a pint of Ear Inn Ale, a shot of Irish whiskey and some great food.

THE HISTORY

The history of the Ear Inn starts, as with so many other bars throughout the US, with some contested historical aspects.

The original building was built in 1817 for a man by the name of James Brown, a Revolutionary War veteran (which is not contested). Legend claims that Brown was an African-American soldier and an aide to none other than George Washington. In fact, some believe it's Brown featured at Washington's side in Emanuel Leutze's 1851 painting titled "Washington Crossing the Delaware".

Though some history of the bar and its original owner has been called into question, what's not disputed is that he opened a successful tobacco shop shortly after construction was completed. In 1833 the building was then sold to Thomas Cloake, who opened a bar on the ground floor. Cloake's bar was the start of one of the longest continually operating bars in American history.

After Thomas Cloake took ownership and installed the bar, the waterfront neighborhood quickly changed. At the time the Hudson River was a mere five feet from the Ear Inn, and the city and its commerce were booming. The bar was frequented by New York's immigrant gang members, river pirates, and visitors looking for female companionship (which could be found in the brothel located on the second floor).

At some point in the mid-19th century the bar became what some described as a "spiritual" establishment, where owner Thomas Cloake brewed beer and corn whiskey (a very rich, double-pot distilled bourbon), and continued to sell most of his products to thirsty sailors, pirates, and immigrant gang members. He also continued to use the top two floors as a brothel, a boarding house and a smuggler's den.

During Prohibition the bar passed itself off as a restaurant while continuing to operate as a speakeasy out of the bottom and second floors. After Prohibition ended the bar was nameless, though sailors and pirates called it "The Green Door," with

the motto "Known from Coast to Coast." Up until 1977 the establishment had a pool table, gambling, and no music except singing by the patrons.

In 1977 the bar was purchased and renamed the Ear Inn so the owners wouldn't have to go through the Landmark Commission's lengthy review of new signs added to historical buildings. To achieve this, the owner simply painted the B on the neon Bar sign to look like an E and the Ear Inn of today was born.

TODAY

Today the Ear Inn is located on the fringes of Soho. If you were to spend the day there you would see the lunch crowd of nearby blue-collar workers give way to the trendy residents of the surrounding neighborhood as day turned night.

They do feature a couple of TVs hanging above the bar, so it's a great place to sit and watch any number of games being televised.

As the day gets later the small building becomes more and more crowded, so get here before 5:00 pm to grab a seat at the bar.

Look around at the artifacts on the wall of the place, much of it spanning the bar's long history. You'll see many references to the second owner, Thomas Cloake. You'll also see many relics and artifacts relating to the sea, all found in the basement or elsewhere in the building. If you notice the many bottles above the bar, know that these were found in the basement as well, and date from as far back as the early 1800s.

THE FOOD

They describe the food as basic, but we must respectfully and heartily disagree. We tried the smoked salmon, chicken pie, steamed mussels, and shrimp salad. All were delicious, decent sized portions, and reasonably priced. If you find yourself at the Ear Inn we feel you can't go wrong with any one or all of these plates (we especially liked the mussels).

THE DRINKS

You won't find any sweet or fruity drinks at the Ear Inn. Their signature drinks, as described by long-serving bartender Gary, are either a pint of the Ear Inn Ale (which we can tell you from personal experience is delicious) or a pint of Guinness and a shot of Jameson. Stop in on the right night and Gary will probably partake in a shot and beer with you and may even give one of his signature toasts.

NEARBY DISTRACTIONS

Intrepid Sea, Air and Space Museum
www.intrepid.org
Pier 86, 12th Ave. and 46th Street New York, NY 10036 (877) 957-7447 (hours vary by season, with shorter hours in the winter. Visit their website for more info).

Originally an Essex-class aircraft carrier built during World War 2, the Intrepid was in service until being decommissioned in 1974. Today she is a world-class museum featuring Sea, Air and Space exhibits including the submarine USS Growler, a Concorde, and the Space Shuttle Enterprise. A short three mile cab ride from the Ear Inn, it's a great opportunity to get close to some of the world's greatest crafts.

New York City Fire Museum
www.nycfiremuseum.org
278 Spring Street New York, NY 10013 (212) 691-1303 (Monday-Sunday 10am-5pm, closed major holidays).

Literally just steps from the Ear Inn, the New York City Fire Museum hosts one of the nation's greatest collections of firefighting memorabilia. Featuring art, artifacts and gear dating back as far as the 18th century, it gives visitors a glimpse into over 300 years of firefighting and the brave men and women who run into burning buildings while everyone else is running out.

Ghostbusters Headquarters
14 North Moore St. New York, NY 10013 (always open. It's actually a real fire station).

Only a half mile from the Ear Inn resides one of the most iconic locations in film history: the Ghostbusters headquarters. Today the building hosts Ladder 8, a company dating back to 1865, and the iconic Ghostbusters sign still hangs in the apparatus bay. For anyone who is familiar with this great New York-based movie, a trip to see this legendary building is well worth the short walk.

THE OLD `76 HOUSE

TAPPAN, NY

110 Main Street
Tappan, NY 10983
(845) 359-5476
http://www.76house.com/
http://youtu.be/eyaYkLT0aEw

Food: Yes
Live Music: Yes
Hours: Monday—Friday, Sunday 11am-9pm,
Saturday 11am-10pm
Type of Bar: Tavern
What to Drink: Try a glass of wine from their extensive selection or an ale from the tap.
Why You Should Go: Drink in the shadow of George Washington, sit in the room where the British first recognized the United States of America.

This little-known jewel is by all accounts the second oldest bar in America, and it could lay claim to the longest running bar in the country. Yet, unlike a lot of other places around the nation, it doesn't tout or flaunt it. Instead, it just kind of waits for you to show up and find out for yourself.

THE HISTORY

Originally built in 1668, the Old '76 House was initially a Public House in the Dutch colony located in current day Tappan, New York.

At the time of its construction a town would not be recognized as such unless it had a place a traveler could spend the evening, get something to eat and drink, provision himself and take care of his horse. Many towns built public houses to meet these needs as well as to be a place where townsfolk could relax, dine, drink, share news, receive and send mail and conduct business. In fact, almost everything related to business at the time was done in the local public house with the exception of legal matters, which were usually completed in the church (the original 1660s church is located across the street).

Old '76 House began life as one of these Public Houses and became a safe haven for Patriots to meet and plot during the years leading up to and during the Revolutionary War.

It is perhaps most well known for its role in the life of Major John Andre, the famous British spy who conspired with Patriot General Benedict Arnold to capture the fort at West Point. He was captured on his way back to British forces and found to be in possession of the blueprints to the fort and plans developed with Benedict Arnold. He was returned to Tappan by American forces and then locked up in the '76 House (known as Mabie's Inn at the time).

He stayed there through the length of his trial at the nearby church until he was convicted and then hanged just up the road on October 2nd, 1780. His last statement: "All I request, gentlemen, is that while I acknowledge the propriety of my sentence, you will bear me witness that I die like a brave man." His remains were later exhumed, and he was buried in Westminster Abbey in London where he is regarded as a Hero. Benedict Arnold escaped to England, where he lived out his life shunned by friends and foes alike.

Less well known but more importantly, the '76 House was also where, on or about May 3rd 1783, England finally recognized the United States as an independent nation when General

Carleton gave Washington the plans for the British evacuation of the country. The meaning is pretty profound if you think about it. Our nation was finally recognized as such in a tavern!

In short, The Old '76 House drips with history.

TODAY

Today the Old '76 House is best described as a pristine, 300-year-old tavern. But it wasn't all that pristine until current owner Robert (Rob) Norden bought the place back in 1987.

Rob and a team of friends set about restoring the place to its former glory immediately after its purchase. Issues included a foundation that wasn't settling uniformly, an original floor and ceiling that were on the brink of collapsing, an inaccurate floor plan that had been established with smaller rooms and even a falsely marked "Andre's prison" that had been erected as a tourist attraction. There was, to put it mildly, a lot of work to do.

It took two years of remodeling to recreate the original public house. In that time 30 tons of foundation clay was removed by hand, and structural renovations were completed using authentic wood found throughout North America. Anything original that could be saved, was, and that includes the bar rail. It was at that very bar rail that none other than George Washington once drank and maybe even ate.

Rob is now happy to compare the '76 House to taverns that existed long ago. They play live music seven nights a week, serve great food and drinks, and take pride in creating an atmosphere that caters to the community. It's warm and comfortable and a great place to while away a Friday or Saturday night.

THE FOOD

The Old '76 House has teamed up with renowned chef Doug Mulholland to present its guests with a blend of traditional colonial foods like Yankee Pot Roast and modern-day dishes like Filet of Escobar.

Their food has won them acclaim in many local foodie magazines and journals, and they're consistently booked for weddings and receptions. Many of Mulholland's dishes feature local and seasonal ingredients and are his take on classic dishes. Try something from the period if you can.

THE DRINKS

Paired with their outstanding menu are their excellent and extensive wine list and a full-service bar. If you drink, do it at the bar standing up (as they would have done) with a hand resting on the large round rail.

Have an ale, glass of wine, or a glass of whiskey neat. Any of these would have been downed by Washington himself, who very well could have been right there where you're standing and at the very same bar rail (kind of humbling, actually).

NEARBY DISTRACTIONS

Major John Andre Monument
42 Andre Hill, Tappan, New York, NY (always open but be mindful of the surrounding neighborhood).

Located just a half mile from the Old '76 House sits the monument to the British Spy Major John Andre. Major Andre was an assistant to British General Clinton, and at Clinton's order traveled to meet American traitor Benedict Arnold to discuss plans for the handing over of West Point. Andre was captured and subsequently tried and sentenced to death. His last request was that his captors bear him witness that he died like a brave man. Today the monument is a solemn reminder of the tragedies of war and the cost of freedom.

Defiant Brewing Co.
www.defiantbrewing.com
6 East Dexter Plaza Pearl River, NY 10965 (845) 920-8602 (brewery and kitchen hours vary, visit website or call).

A short six mile drive from Old '76 House will get you to Defiant Brewing Company. Stop in for a tour and sample of their high-quality craft beer. They also recently opened a kitchen serving brisket, pulled pork and ribs served by the pound, so you decide on how big you want your portion.

Tallman Mountain State Park
www.nysparks.com
(hours vary by season).

Just three miles away from the Old '76 House is Tallman

Mountain State Park, offering an opportunity to view some of New York's wooded and marshlands while enjoying hiking trails, cross-country skiing and picnic areas. Spend a few hours exploring New York's "wilder" side, and then head to Old '76 House to try some outstanding food and drink at the bar rail at which George Washington once stood.

OTHER NOTABLE AREA BARS

Pete's Tavern

**129 East 18th Street New York, NY 10003 (212) 473-7676
(Monday-Tuesday, Sunday 11am-11:45pm,
Wednesday-Saturday 11am-12:45am).**

Pete's claims to be the oldest continuously operating bar in New York City, a claim that's hard to pin down. It became a bar in 1864, making it younger than some of the others, but it is the only one that is documented as serving through Prohibition, which is how they get their claim—continuously operating. True or not, this is a haven for locals, students and tourists. This is where the famous short story, "The Gift of the Magi" was written by O. Henry, and it boasts a long line of celebrities and famous personalities through its doors.

White Horse Tavern

**567 Hudson Street Manhattan, NY 10014 (212) 989-3956
(Monday-Thursday and Sunday 11am-2am,
Friday-Saturday 11am-4am).**

This was a quiet bar opened in 1880 to serve the longshoremen and seaside merchants and workers until writers and Bohemian artists began frequenting the place in the 1950s. The scene changed fairly quickly, especially when Dylan Thomas became so famous, and then the bar became a trendy spot for locals and tourists.

PJ Clarke's
915 3rd Ave. New York, NY 10022 (212) 317-1616 (Monday-Sunday 11:30am-4am).

Opened in 1884 as a saloon for Irish locals, PJ Clarke's has become a favorite watering hole for New York residents and tourists alike. Its claim to fame is that the place simply didn't close. Anywhere else this wouldn't seem like quite an accomplishment, but considering the growth of skyscrapers in the surrounding area it's actually amazing to see this place still exists. They claim to have served through Prohibition (which they probably did), and then didn't allow women in until the 1960s. Much of the history hangs on the walls, though, and you'll find a picture gallery of the who's who of New York City.

PHILADELPHIA

The City of Brotherly Love has a great past that anyone with any interest in history will appreciate. Not only that, but a couple of places have kept their personality despite the growth of the city into the monster metropolis it is now.

There's a certain sense of wonder you get when visiting this city that comes from knowing all of the events that took place here that shaped our country's future. But even more so, knowing how much the bar scene actually contributed to that shaping, drinking here is itself a rite for anyone that appreciates a good saloon.

Many don't know that the Declaration of Independence was written in a tavern in this city. Thomas Jefferson hunched over a small table in the Indian Queen Tavern for three days, drinking ale and Madeira wine while penning what was to become one of the most famous pieces of writing in history.

And just down the street from the Indian Queen you'll find the birthplace of the United State Marine Corps, or at least a marker denoting as much. The marker is actually for the Tun Tavern. That's right: the USMC was born in a tavern. The owner of the place was made chief recruiting officer for the newly formed USMC by the Continental Congress in 1775. And so he naturally set up a table in his own place and began getting his customers—drunk or sober—to sign up for the Corps.

Just about every important event that happened in this city had something to do with booze and bars. The politicking that went into our nation's founding? That didn't take place in Independence Hall; it took place in the taverns over ale and rum punches.

And in fact, one of the biggest parties in history was thrown in one of the bars you can visit today. On September 17th, 1787, after signing the US Constitution, the 55 delegates of the Continental Congress (plus General George Washington) met for dinner and a celebration at City Tavern. In the course of the evening the Founding Fathers put away 100 bottles of wine, 34 bottles of beer, 8 bottles of whiskey, 8 bottles of hard cider, and 7 bowls of rum punch. What makes this event even funnier is that the tavern-keeper added 2% to the bill for "damages" done. This place is, of course, a Bucket List Bar™; however we don't suggest trying to reenact this historic event.

TRANSPORTATION: Capital Dispatch Inc. (215) 235-2200 (Monday-Sunday 24 hours). Quaker City Cab (267) 298-1088 (Monday-Sunday 24 hours).

THE CITY TAVERN

PHILADELPHIA, PA

138 South 2nd Street
Philadelphia, PA 19106
(215) 413-1443
http://www.citytavern.com/
http://youtu.be/Wf6mlZ__724

Food: Yes
Live Music: Yes
Hours: Monday—Thursday, Sunday 11:30am-9pm,
Friday—Saturday 11:30am-10pm
Type of Bar: Tavern
What to Drink: A Shrub, a Tavern Cooler or Ales of the
Revolution.
Why You Should Go: This tavern was the most impor-
tant place in the city of Philadelphia during the founding
of our nation.

From its opening in 1773 until it was demolished in 1854 and rebuilt again in 1976, the City Tavern has likely experienced more historic events than any other building in the United States.

THE HISTORY

Originally built for the "convenience and credit of city" the City Tavern in Philadelphia was established in 1773. Shortly after it opened its doors, John Adams attended a meeting of the First Continental Congress there and it was described as "the most genteel tavern in America."

Paul Revere rode to the Tavern on more than one occasion, reporting news of the Boston Tea Party and later of the closing of Boston's port by the British.

The Second Continental Congress began meeting in the Tavern in May of 1775, with members meeting every Saturday. Eight of them formed a "table" and dined there daily.

Benjamin Franklin practically lived here, and John Adams and George Washington met for the first time in the same room where you can now eat and drink.

Things changed for the Tavern when British General Cornwallis marched his troops directly to it on September 24th, 1777. British officers assigned quarters in the Tavern had weekly balls. Two single officers advertised for "a young woman to work in the capacity of a housekeeper, who can occasionally put her hand to anything. Extravagant wages will be given, and no character [references] required."

There are books devoted to the history of this amazing place. What's important for this book, though, was that this was the place to have food and drink in Philadelphia. In fact, on the night of September 17th, 1787 the members of the Continental Congress, chose the City Tavern as their spot in which to throw one of the most infamous parties ever recorded.

The 55 members of the Congress (plus George Washington) at that soirée went through 100 bottles of wine, 22 bottles of porter, 12 bottles of beer, eight bottles of whiskey, eight bottles of hard cider and seven bowls of spiked punch.

TODAY

The original City Tavern was demolished in 1854 but in 1948 the government designated parts of downtown Philadelphia as National Historic Parks. Part of the reconstruction included the rebuilding of the City Tavern, and construction was completed just in time for the nation's bicentennial. The tavern was rebuilt as an exact replica of the original, right down to the seating, the room layout and, of course, the bar (called the dispensary at the time).

Proprietor and Head Chef Walter Staib has converted the City Tavern into an award-winning restaurant with seven dining rooms, three wine cellars, and an award-winning menu inspired by 18th-century American cuisine. Himself a James Beard Foundation Nominee and Emmy Award-winner, Staib has poured himself into returning the City Tavern to its previous glory. From the Colonial food and drinks, to the decor and the furniture, sitting down for a meal or having a cocktail is like being transported back in time to the days of our Founding Fathers. No other place we have visited has been able to give us such an authentic feel.

The place to retire to is the dispensary. This small room hosts a collection of booths, a couple of benches and a few tables and chairs. It's from this little room that period drinks are mixed and served.

THE FOOD

The food at the City Tavern is some of the most unique (not to mention some of the best) we have ever tried. Chef Walter Staib has spent considerable time and effort researching true colonial food and period menus, and he presents his findings and recipes in his critically acclaimed television show, "A Taste of History."

The same enthusiasm evident in his show has been put into his menu at the City Tavern.

A great starter for any meal is his West Indies Pepperpot Soup. This was a colonial favorite (George Washington served it to his troops after crossing the Delaware) and consists of beef, taro roots, and greens.

Also try Chef Staib's Veal and Herb Sausage "Munchner Style." Consisting of handmade veal sausage, Pennsylvania Dutch-style sauerkraut, mashed potatoes and Dijon mustard, it is simply delicious (especially when paired with his beer).

THE DRINKS

Chef Staib also researched and reintroduced period beer and cocktails at the City Tavern to go with his period cuisine.

No visit to the Tavern is complete without trying the Ales of the Revolution sampler. The sampler is four different kinds of beers, each featuring original recipes from great brewers such as George Washington and Thomas Jefferson. Each is unique, all are great, and most are toned down slightly due to the high alcohol content in the original recipes.

After finishing off the beer, move on to the Rum Shrub. The Shrub dates back to the 1700s and was originally designed to hide flaws in rum as well as take advantage of fruit that started to turn before it was used. It's a mixture of fruit juice vinegar (called shrub), sugar (or other sweetener like simple syrup), water, and rum.

We can also recommend the City Tavern Cooler. Another

period drink it's made with peach brandy, West Indies rum, whiskey, and then topped with apple cider and stirred with a cinnamon stick. The spirits mix amazingly well while the sweetness of the cider tones down the harshness of the liquor.

http://youtu.be/mnSIsVdNuQY

http://youtu.be/Umj0XKea5Ak

NEARBY DISTRACTIONS

Tun Tavern Memorial Marker

Sansom Street & South Front Street Philadelphia, PA (always open).

Located less than a quarter of a mile from City Tavern is the site of the legendary Tun Tavern. It was at this very location that on November 10th, 1775, the United States Marine Corps was born. The owner of the Tun was appointed Recruiting Officer by the Second Continental Congress, and so naturally he began signing up his patrons. Unfortunately, the tavern burned down in 1781, and today most of the location is covered by I-95. All that remains of this storied tavern is the historical marker, which makes a great photo opp.

Independence Hall

www.nps.gov/inde, 520 Chestnut Street Philadelphia, PA 19106 (215) 965-2305 (Monday-Sunday 9am-5pm except Christmas day).

It's in this very building that on July 4th, 1776, the United States Declaration of Independence was approved by the Continental Congress. This is where America finally declared its independence from England, and this is where America was born. At only a half mile from the City Tavern, no visit to the area is complete without a visit to this historic building.

Liberty Bell Center

www.nps.gov/inde/liberty-bell-center.htm, 138 South 2nd Street Philadelphia, PA 19106 (215) 965-2305 (Monday-Sunday 9am-5pm except Christmas day).

Few iconic symbols stir as much within Americans as the Liberty Bell. A long-lasting symbol of American independence, revolutionary progress and the American spirit, it's well worth the usually long wait in line for a glimpse of this American treasure.

MCGILLIN'S OLDE ALE HOUSE

PHILADELPHIA, PA

1310 Drury Street
Philadelphia, PA 19107
(215) 735-5562
http://www.mcgillins.com/
http://youtu.be/qNjMvs94kgU

Food: Yes
Live Music: Yes
Hours: Monday—Sunday 11am-2am
Type of Bar: Pub
What to Drink: McGillin's 1860 IPA
Why You Should Go: A bar since 1860, a staple of
Philadelphia, plus the century-old gallery of signs and
advertising from Philadelphia-area businesses.

This is one of those places that you've probably seen, heard or read about. It's a piece of American history, not to mention a great success story about the influx of Irish immigrants fleeing to the States in the 1800s.

THE HISTORY

McGillin's opened its doors in 1860, making it over 150 years old, one of the oldest bars in America and Philadelphia's oldest continuously operating bar. Though it originally opened as The Bell In Hand, its patrons simply called it McGillin's after owner, William McGillin. Called "Pa" by his patrons, McGillin was an Irish immigrant who came to the United States because of the Irish Potato Famine in the mid-19th century. Pa used the upper levels of the building to house himself, his wife and his 13 children. As the bar quickly became popular William expanded, taking over the oyster house next door, the back alley/washroom and eventually even McGillin's own house upstairs.

Unfortunately, Pa McGillin passed away in 1901, leaving his wife, Catherine "Ma" McGillin, to take over the management of the bar and restaurant. A smart businesswoman, Catherine continued Pa's renovation and expansion plans, and continued to run the place until the mid-1930s.

Part of her tenure encompassed Prohibition, when she famously locked the front door and vowed that no one would enter through it until the Volstead Act was repealed (not realizing it would take 14 years). True to her vow she used the backdoor as the entrance to the restaurant (with speakeasy upstairs).

Ma passed away in 1937, at which time her daughter Mercedes took over operation until 1958 when she sold it to two brothers, Henry Spaniak and Joe Shepaniak (for some reason the brothers spelled their last names differently).

While always a popular neighborhood bar it was in the 1950s that it really started to come into its own thanks to a new crowd of patrons. Celebrities like Will Rogers, the Marx Brothers, Vincent Price, and Tennessee Williams would visit McGillin's for a drink, some food, and entertainment. As the number of celebrities increased so did the bar's popularity.

TODAY

Today the bar remains in the Spaniak/Shepaniak family and is run by Mary Ellen and her husband, Chris Mullins: Henry Spaniak's daughter and son-in-law. It's still frequented by celebrities, like Robin Williams, Will Ferrell, Bam Margera, local sports stars, and musicians in town for concerts.

Widely considered Philadelphia's best Irish bar, and on the top list of many magazines and culinary journals (like "Gourmet", among others), McGillin's looks like what you'd imagine a 19th-century Irish bar *should* look like. It'll seem almost familiar at first—the walls covered in bric-a-brac, the friendly crowd and the gleaming wood of the bar. It'll take a minute for you to realize that just about every chain, wannabe Irish pub and restaurant is copying this place in their bland formulas.

The real deal is worth it, though. The bric-a-brac on the walls isn't really random; it's been collected over 150 years—like the old assortment of liquor licenses behind the bar—and has a lot of significance to Philadelphia (especially the collection of advertising and signs belonging to once-landmark-stores like Wanamaker's).

THE FOOD

From Mile High Meatloaf to shepherd's pie, mussels, steaks and other Irish favorites, McGillin's features some excellent dishes. Most meals come with a bowl of soup from their self-serve station and they offer a different special every night of the week.

Most would describe the fare as comfort food, but they do spend an immense amount of time to make it even more comfortable. Many of the herbs are fresh from the owner's personal herb garden. They also take pains to get fresh fruit and vegetables, like tomatoes from nearby New Jersey, and fresh seafood.

We didn't sample any food ourselves, but owner Chris Mullins will gladly tell you what's in season and is best for that evening's meal.

THE DRINKS

McGillin's has a full-service bar that can mix up just about anything you could want, but their real specialties are their craft and custom-made beers. They're happy to point out that they were the first place in Philadelphia to embrace local craft beers, and so it's only fitting they commissioned a local brewery to produce some beers just for them.

McGillin's has three house beers: McGillin's Real Ale, McGillin's Genuine Lager and McGillin's 1860 IPA. The lager and the ale are both outstanding beers, but the real treat is their IPA. Originally created as part of the 150th anniversary celebration in 2010, the IPA is unfiltered, making it similar to the beers drunk in the 1800s. Unsurprisingly, the recipe is secret, but we do know that it contains multiple hop varieties, including Centennial and Amarillo.

McGillin's IPA is an outstanding beer available both on tap at the bar and at a select few distributors around Philadelphia and is the must-try drink when you visit.

NEARBY DISTRACTIONS

Masonic Library and Museum
www.pagrandlodge.org,
1 North Broad Street Philadelphia, PA 19107 (215) 988-1900
(tour times vary; refer to website for additional information).

With origins dating back to the 16th century (and possibly even earlier) the Freemasons played a significant role in American History. Take the opportunity to visit this iconic Freemason lodge to get a new and unique look into the founding of our nation and the great men who molded it.

Simeone Automotive Museum
www.simeonemuseum.org
6825 Norwitch Drive Philadelphia, PA 19153 (215) 365-7233
(Tuesday-Friday 10am-6pm, Saturday-Sunday 10am-4pm).

A short five-mile drive from McGillin's will deliver you to the Simeone Automotive Museum. Featuring race cars dating back to the early 1900s, the museum is not only unique in its cars but also in the fact that many of the cars are still driven on

Demonstration Days. Open to the public this is one of the few if not the only place you can still hear, see and smell these classic cars as they tear around the track.

The Rocky Statue
Kelly Drive Philadelphia, PA 19130 (always open).

The statue of the fictional Rocky character is one of the city's most notable landmarks. An immortalization of the Rocky character, it was built to pay tribute to the underdog, much like the US was when it declared its independence from Britain. Only two miles away from McGillin's, it is a perfect stop for a free photo op and a run up the fabled stairs.

OTHER NOTABLE AREA BARS

Khyber Pass Pub
56 South 2nd Street Philadelphia, PA 19106 (215) 238-5888 (Monday-Sunday 11am-2pm).

This is typically called a "cozy dive bar," which really makes no sense. Maybe they mean small? Not threatening? We're not sure, but it is somewhat of a legend in this city. The selling point for historic bar lovers is that there has reportedly been a drinking establishment at this location since 1876, making it the third oldest location in Philadelphia (even if it did change names over the decades).

Dock Street Brewery
701 South 50th Street Philadelphia, PA 19143 (215) 726-2337(Monday-Wednesday 3pm-10pm, Thursday 3pm-11pm, Friday 11:30am-12am, Saturday 12pm-12am).

Founded in 1985 this is the first microbrewery in Philly and one of the first in the United States. It's a notable bar to visit simply because of this. The owners did something new and different, and now all of these new craft microbreweries opening up are a result of their legacy. Great place to go for some seriously good beer and even better history.

BOSTON AREA

There are few cities in America with the history boasted by Boston. Founded by Puritans in 1630, it's come to represent much of what we think of when we think of the early years of the United States. Not only was it one of the first colonies, but it was also one of the most important, and was a leading center for rebellion and uprising during the Revolutionary War.

As can be imagined this early history has itself played a role in shaping how the city has turned out. And as a result Boston identifies itself as much for its history as for its modern contributions to the country. And though it strives to be taken seriously for its current drive to be a focus of the high-tech industry in New England, it's also constantly reminding visitors of its past and place in history at every opportunity.

For the traveler looking for a new place to drink, a welcoming pub, or a slice of early American bar life, Boston is a great place to get lost in.

Those who remember the 80s might recollect Cheers as being here. It was. It was a genuine imitation of a not-very-old bar you can still go to today.

And as far as the old, historic bars, there are still a few worthy of your money.

What you have to remember about this city, though, is that so many historic characters traipsed through here during the most important moments of our history. And that pretty much means that everyone claims the presence of historic figures. That's why if you go anywhere in the city short of a Walmart you'll probably see a plaque claiming that John Adams, Sam Adams, or even Paul Revere had been there/drank there/evacuated himself there.

We don't want to cast any doubts on the authenticity of any of these places, but do take these claims with a grain of salt (unless we tell you).

TRANSPORTATION: Metro Cab (617) 782-5500 (Monday-Sunday 9am-5pm), Abrassador Brattle Cab (617) 492-1100 (Monday-Sunday 12am-12am) In Newport: Leisure Limousine (401) 683-2683 (Monday-Friday 9am-5pm).

WARREN TAVERN

CHARLESTOWN, MA

2 Pleasant Street
Charlestown, MA
(617) 241-8142
http://www.warrentavern.com
http://youtu.be/UO0qJmM6rfE

Food: Yes
Live Music: No
Hours: Monday—Friday 11:30am-1am,
Saturday—Sunday 10:30am-1am
Type of Bar: Tavern
What to Drink: Samuel Adams
Why You Should Go: Founded in 1780 it's one of the
oldest original taverns in the country (not moved from
some other location or rebuilt later with the same name),
and the most authentic in Boston.

To walk within the walls of the Warren Tavern is to walk in the footsteps of Washington, Revere and other Founding Fathers. And to drink here—or should we say, to get drunk here—is to honor our very first president, who himself passed out a time or two at this watering hole.

THE HISTORY

Just feet from the historic Freedom Trail, tracing the history of our country's founding through Boston, sits the Warren Tavern. Erected in 1780 in Charlestown, Massachusetts, today it is over 225 years old and is the oldest and most celebrated bar in the area.

Rumored to have been one of the first buildings built after the British burned down Charlestown following the legendary Battle of Bunker Hill (1775), this place simply oozes American history and is what we feel truly embodies what a tavern should be.

Captain Eliphelet Newell, himself a participant in the Boston Tea Party, built and named the tavern after the legendary Patriot leader Doctor Joseph Warren, who was killed at Bunker Hill.

After construction was completed the tavern quickly became Paul Revere's favorite watering hole. George Washington is also known to have stopped by on more than one occasion and even over-indulged in a drink or two.

As it was intended when it was originally built and through-out its history the tavern has been a local watering hole, where one could stop in for a drink, a meal and be updated on local and national news.

TODAY

Today the Warren Tavern is a cornerstone of the city of Charlestown and its residents. It continues its tradition of being a true tavern where locals and tourists alike mingle in the historic structure sharing ideas, arguing differing views, conversing about local, national and international events and simply having a good time. The tavern is exactly what Captain Newell had intended when he originally built it, and we honestly believe that if either Newell or Warren himself were to walk into the bar today he would not only approve but would also feel right at home.

Upon entering, a tall person might feel a bit claustrophobic. The low-hung ceilings were typical for the time period, and built that way to keep heat in during the winters. The place is

inviting and the bar is scattered with a handful of regulars. This is a great place to watch a game or just while away the hours.

THE FOOD

The Warren Tavern is famous for its Tavern Burger, which features house garlic-herb cream cheese (to top it off smear on some of their house garlic-mustard). Their mustard, which you can buy by the jar, is something of legend, and you should definitely buy a few jars to take home—if you like mustard, that is. But beyond the burger the must-try item is the clam chowder.

There was little doubt in our minds we were in for a treat when the Warren Tavern's manager John told us he would put their clam chowder against any in the nation without hesitation. And we have no hesitation when we tell you that the clam chowder at the Warren Tavern is the best we've ever had. Don't get a cup—it won't be enough; Get a bowl and love every bite. You can thank us later.

THE DRINKS

The Warren includes a full bar that serves just about every cocktail you can imagine. Their beer selection is also regional and seasonal, so there's little doubt that you'll find something you like.

For us though, it had to be a Sam Adams. Boston Beer Company is just across the bridge, and Sam Adams Lager and Ale permeate this area of the country. What better beer to drink

than one that was named for one of our Founding Fathers while sitting in such a historic setting—a setting that also entertained the men we've read about in history books.

NEARBY DISTRACTIONS

Bunker Hill Monument
Monument Square, Charlestown, MA 02129, (617) 242-5641 (Monday-Sunday 9am-5pm).

Only four blocks northeast of Warren Tavern is the site of the famous Battle of Bunker Hill, ironically enough not on Bunker Hill but on Breed's Hill. The granite obelisk and visitor's center mark the sites of one of the most famous and earliest battles of the Revolutionary War in 1775. It was here that Dr. Joseph Warren lost his life and the Patriots infused the colonies with their bravado.

USS Constitution

Building 22, Charlestown Navy Yard Boston, MA 02129, (617) 426-1812 (November 1-March 1, Thursday-Sunday 10am-6pm, April 1-September 30 Tuesday-Sunday 10am-6pm, October 1-October 31 Tuesday-Sunday 10am-4pm).

Located about 10 long blocks east of the Warren Tavern sits Old Ironsides herself: the USS Constitution. Launched in 1797, she's still an active US Navy warship and crewed by sailor and Marine tour-guides in period costume. It's actually really stunning to view this ship and see how the sailors used to live and fight.

Samuel Adams (Boston Beer Company) Brewery Tour

30 Germania Street, Boston, MA 02130 (617) 368-5080 (Monday-Thursday 10am-3pm, Fridays 10am-5:30pm, Saturdays 10am-3pm).

You'll need transportation to get here, but it'll be worth it. You'll see how the biggest independent brewer in America operates and get a couple of beer samples to boot. The beer is found all over the area anyway, so you might as well make the trip to its origin while you're here.

WHITE HORSE TAVERN

NEWPORT, RI

26 Marlborough Street
Newport, RI 02840
(401) 849-3600
http://www.whitehorsetavern.us/
http://youtu.be/c3ZcmgmXU6o

Food: Yes
Live Music: No
Hours: Monday—Thursday 11:30am-9pm, Friday—
Saturday 11:30am-10pm, Sunday 11am-9pm
What do drink: Dark and Stormy™
Type of Bar: Tavern
Why You Should Go: Oldest bar in America.

Going to the White Horse Tavern should feel like a pilgrimage for anyone with an interest in the history of bars in America. This place harkens back to the oldest days of our country, when the tavern was the heart and soul of a community.

THE HISTORY

Constructed in 1652 as a lavish two-story residence for the Brinley family, it was sold to William Mayes Sr. and converted into a tavern in 1673. Stop for a moment and consider that: this place was a tavern over 100 years before the US was a country.

Besides a tavern, the establishment was also used for large assemblies, as a courthouse and even as city hall during the early years of Newport's existence.

William Mayes Jr., a notorious pirate, took over operation in the early 1700s after returning home with bounty rumored to have come from his adventures on the high seas. Hated by and a constant embarrassment to local British officials, he was loved and protected by the townspeople. Rumor has it the tavern played host to a multitude of pirate gatherings, rum trades and other illicit activities.

Eventually the establishment was sold to Jonathan Nichols who is responsible for naming the tavern "The White Horse Tavern."

During the Revolutionary War it was used by British troops for quarters. Rather than stay with Hessian mercenaries, Walter Nichols (son of Jonathan and owner at the time) fled with his family. Once the war ended, they promptly returned to set up shop.

The tavern was finally turned into a boarding house in the late 1800s and quickly fell into a state of disrepair. In the 1950s the Van Beuren family made a sizeable donation to the Preservation Society of Newport County for the purpose of restoring the building to once again be used as a tavern and restaurant. The White Horse reopened and has been in constant operation since 1957.

TODAY

Today the White Horse Tavern continues its rich tradition, serving great drinks and fine food on both of its floors. The building itself, though it has some modern additions, still retains its classic and traditional feel. From its large fireplaces to its antique furniture, period paintings and prints, this place feels like it's straight out of the late 1600s. It's easy to imagine colonials and even pirates stepping through its front doors, grabbing a drink at the bar and then sitting at the fireplace to warm up from the cold outside.

Though the building is predominantly restaurant, the bar is still a prominent feature. In fact there are two of them, one upstairs that resembles more of a traditional tavern-style bar, and the bar downstairs—the main bar—that has a few scattered tables, stools and is flanked by a huge fireplace, at one time used for kitchen duty. This room is where you should make your stand.

THE FOOD

The White Horse is really about fine dining, and we have to admit, it's pretty good. Their clam chowder is outstanding, their Georges Bank Scallops are grand, but the must-try is

their Individual Beef Wellington. Wrapped in a puff pastry, the seared prime tenderloin melts in your mouth and is exceptionally delicious.

THE DRINKS

The White Horse features a full bar with a long list of outstanding cocktails, but their most popular is the Dark and Stormy™.

Consisting of ginger beer, a float of Myer's Rum, and garnished with a lime and served in a highball glass, the drink is a popular classic in many British Commonwealth countries. Its appearance as the dark rum slowly sinks into the ginger beer is similar to what one may see as the sun sets on a dark and stormy night, hence the name. It is a must-try on your visit to the White Horse.

NEARBY DISTRACTIONS

12 Meter Charters
www.12metercharters.com
49 Bowen's Wharf 3rd Floor Newport, RI 02840 (401) 851-1216
(operating hours vary by season and charter types).

Have a few hours to kill and want to give sailing a try? If so, then check out 12 Meter Charters just half a mile from the White Horse Tavern. Featuring multiple former America's Cup sailboats and requiring no prior sailing background, it will give you a chance to experience New England sailing at its finest.

Newport History Tours

www.newporthistorytours.org
(401) 846-0813 (operating hours and locations
vary by tour and season).

Interested in taking a step back into Newport's past and discov-
ering where pirates lived, criminals were punished, riots took
place, remarkable entrepreneurship occurred and what life was
like for Newport's original settlers? If so, check out the Newport
Historical Society's long list of historical tours. They'll help put
the area into a better context and get you in the right frame of
mind for drinks later at the White Horse Tavern.

Fishing Charters

www.flippingoutcharters.com (401) 529-2267,
www.newportriwatersports.com (401) 849-4820,
www.flahertycharters.com (401) 848-5554.

If you're in town for more than a night you might want to try
your hand at catching some of New England's legendary fish.
There are a number of charters to choose from, but for starters
give one of the local fishing charters listed here a try. In the
waters off of Newport you'll have the chance to hook into a
shark, squid or a legendary striper.

OTHER NOTABLE AREA BARS

The Green Dragon
**11 Marshall Street Boston, MA 02108 (617) 367-0055
(Monday-Sunday 11am-2am).**

This is an imitation of the real and important landmark tavern that was frequented by so many of the Patriots leading up to the Revolutionary War—in fact the real one was where the Boston Tea Party was planned (probably after too many shots of rum). This one, on the other hand, is really nothing like it. Never mind the fact it was built in the '90s (1990s that is), but this one is more of an Irish-type pub and probably little like the real one at all. However it's fun to say you were here, plus the locale is boozer central, so if the scene is lousy you can walk across the alley to the other notable.

The Bell in Hand Tavern
**45 Union Street Boston, MA 02108 (617) 227-2098
(Monday-Sunday 11:30am-2am).**

Emblazoned across the top of the first floor are the worn gilded wood letters proclaiming "America's Oldest Tavern." It's not. Its claim lies in the fine print of *continuously operating*, meaning it's been going since 1795, though even this claim is dubious since it moved from the original 1795 home blocks away to its current residence sometime in the late 1800s, and surely they had to close for a period then. But in any case they do have pieces of the original place in here, like a section of the original bar and the original sign. It's worth it to be close to many other Irish pubs and close to the water. Not truly authentic but still a fun time.

CHICAGO AREA

Chicago's long bar history—not to mention its stellar brewing and distilling history—was cut short by the great fire of 1871. The fire, which ravaged the city and destroyed over 3.3 square miles in the heart of Chicago, left over 100,000 people homeless and (more to our point), leveled most every old saloon there was.

People rebuilt, of course, but a result of the fire was that the city forbade wooden structures, and so many of the glorious old city bars were never to be rebuilt.

That aside, though, Chicago's historic boozing was unharmed. This city, after all, was home to Brunswick, famous for its bowling legacy, but in the 1800s (and even early 1900s) was the primary supplier of ornate, hardwood bars shipped across the country.

Brunswick bars ended up in the most obscure of places, including Tombstone, Arizona, and Goodsprings, Nevada. Ultimately, if you see the Duke belly up to a big beautiful bar in an old Hollywood Western, it was modeled after the furniture coming out of Chicago.

Perhaps what comes to mind for many when they think of Chicago is Prohibition. After all, this was home to some of the more notorious bootlegging mobs in the country at the time.

Not only that, the place was absolutely rotten with speakeasies and blind tigers. In fact it's estimated that there were about a thousand of these illegal bars in the city at any given time during Prohibition.

And this is what makes the bars in this city great. We're not going here to find the founding of our country, as we would in Philly or New England, or even to soak up the atmosphere of the grogshops and alehouses of the 19th century like we would in New York City. Here we're looking at bars that had some kind of tie to America's dumbest of laws—the Volstead Act. Plus, to be safe we throw in a few historic and hidden gems you have to try to make the trip really worth it.

TRANSPORTATION: Chicago Carriage Cab Co. (312) 791-1273 (Monday-Sunday 12am-11:30pm). Sun Taxi (773) 736-3883 (Monday-Sunday 24hrs).

THE GREEN MILL

CHICAGO, IL

4802 N. Broadway Ave.
Chicago, IL 60640
(773) 878-5552
http://www.greenmilljazz.com
http://youtu.be/0oHCAYX8-lw

Food: No
Live Music: Yes
Hours: Monday—Sunday 12pm-4am
Type of Bar: Speakeasy
What to Drink: Gin martini
Why You Should Go: Capone's personal speakeasy, perfectly preserved and ready for him to visit.

The Green Mill was originally a dance and music venue, similar to Paris' Moulin Rouge (Moulin Rouge translated from French means Red Mill). During Prohibition it was a speakeasy and a favorite hangout of Al Capone (you can still sit in his booth today). It's now a nod to the roaring '20s with original period furniture and décor, and it is also a premiere venue for seeing top jazz acts perform live.

THE HISTORY

The Green Mill was opened in 1907 (as Pop Morse's Roadhouse) originally as a stopping place for funeral goers in transit to or from St. Boniface's Cemetery not far away. The area was in a state of transformation during the early 1900s and considered part of the up-and-coming entertainment district of Chicago.

New owners purchased the roadhouse in 1910 with the hopes of recreating Paris' famous Moulin Rouge, notorious at the time for its excess—free-flowing champagne, constantly changing décor and dancing girls in provocative outfits.

When the Green Mill opened in 1910 it was considerably larger than what you will find standing today, taking up almost an entire city block and containing a huge ballroom, stage for dancing girls, multiple lounges, live music, and a restaurant. The original entrance is still found next door: look for the windmill carved into granite right above the entrance to (at the time of writing) a Mexican food restaurant.

After the Volstead Act was passed in 1919, the place—in its original size—was no longer sustainable. However, the Green Mill was promptly downsized and transformed into a speakeasy.

Sometime during the 1920s one of Al Capone's henchmen, "Machine-gun" Jack McGurn, gained a 25% stake in the club. McGurn as a person was pretty rotten; he ordered a gruesome hit on one of the Green Mill's performers and—according to many—masterminded the St. Valentine's Day massacre.

Once Prohibition ended the place remained a destination for jazz acts and fine cocktails, which still holds true today.

TODAY

Today the bar is over 100 years old and is what many consider both the best jazz club in the US and the crown jewel of Chicago's Uptown. When you walk in you feel like you've just been deposited into a 1920s speakeasy: all of the elements are

present—dim lighting, paneled paintings on the walls, green velvet booths and some of the best jazz bands in the area.

While we were there we both commented that we wouldn't be surprised to see Al Capone himself come strolling in the door and take a seat at his favorite booth. It is a place one can go to enjoy either a top-dollar martini or a cold draft of Schlitz while listening to great live acts.

The Green Mill has a long and rich history of great music and entertainment, and its stage has legends perform almost nightly. Their list of acts includes Joe E. Lewis, Frank Sinatra, the Mighty Blue Kings, David Liebman, Kurt Elling, Sheila Jordan and Mark Murphy, to name just a few. It also has the longest running poetry slam in all of Chicago (every Sunday night, when a $6 cover will get you in to see amateur poets perform). If you come for the live music, arrive early (it was getting crowded at 8:00 pm) to get a table, booth or seat at the bar. However, be prepared to wait, because the first act may not go on until 11:00 pm or later.

When you get here you've got to ask for Capone's special booth. Legend has it that when Capone arrived the band would stop playing whatever set they were playing and start up Capone's favorite song, "Rhapsody Blues." He would then take a seat at his favorite booth located at the end of the bar and opposite the side door leading to Lawrence Street (this gave him good views of both entrances and allowed him to see who was coming or going). Arrive early if you want the booth since, unsurprisingly, it is the most popular table in the bar.

THE DRINKS

The Green Mill sells more of a drink specific to Chicago than anywhere else in the world: Malort. Malort is a liqueur made with grapefruit and wormwood—the ingredient also found in absinthe. It's certainly an acquired taste and not for everyone (think grapefruit plus bile).

They're also very traditional when it comes to their cocktail menu (in fact, they don't have one). The Green Mill is of the opinion that if you don't know what it is you want, you probably shouldn't be drinking it. We suggest a classic drink, the gin martini. We like gin because that's what they would have put in the drink in the '20s. A classic drink for a classic bar.

NEARBY DISTRACTIONS

The Aragon Entertainment Center

1106 West Lawrence Avenue, Chicago, IL 60640 (773) 561-9500 (operating times vary by show; check their website or call).

Since you're in Chicago's historic uptown theater district, why not try and catch a show at the Aragon. Built in 1926 for a healthy sum of two million dollars, it was modeled to resemble a Spanish palace courtyard complete with crystal chandeliers, mosaic tiles, terra-cotta ceilings, balconies and grand arches. Acts vary, but stopping by the Green Mill before and/or after a show will make for a fun-filled night.

Riviera Theater

4746 North Racine Avenue, Chicago, IL 60640 (773) 275-6800 (operating times and shows vary throughout the year; check their website or call).

Originally built in 1917 as a movie theater, it was transformed into a private nightclub in 1986. Featuring a long list of up-and-coming as well as legendary performers and entertainers, the Riviera is another gem in Chicago's uptown theater district.

Spacca Napoli

**1769 West Sunnyside Avenue, Chicago, IL 60640 (773) 878-2420
(Tuesday 5pm-9pm, Wednesday-Thursday 11:30am-3pm,
5pm-9pm, Friday 11:30am-3pm, 5pm-10pm,
Saturday 11:30am-10pm, Sunday 12pm-9pm).**

Just a short one mile jaunt from the Green Mill is Spacca Napoli Pizzeria. Step out of Chicago's deep dish norm and try some authentic Italian wood-fired pizza before heading to a show or to the Green Mill for a few drinks.

SIMON'S TAVERN
CHICAGO, IL

5210 N. Clark St.
Chicago, IL 60640
(575) 878-0894
http://www.simonstavern.com
http://youtu.be/fwRj3uPChQ8

Food: Yes
Live Music: Yes
Hours: Monday—Friday 11am-2am, Saturday
11am-3am
Type of Bar: Pub
What to Drink: Glogg or a shot of Aquavit
Why You Should Go: Original speakeasy, Swedish culture, Chicago history, Nickel Tour.

Thanks to a recommendation, we found ourselves at a place that markets itself with fish drinking martinis, Viking paraphernalia and Swedish flags. Simon's Tavern is a little -known jewel in the heart of the small section of Chicago called Andersonville.

THE HISTORY

Simon's Tavern is named after its founder, Swedish immigrant Simon Lumberg. The history of the bar is really the history of Simon, his immigration to the United States, and the neighborhood bar he had always dreamed of owning.

Simon emigrated from Sweden in the early 1900s and joined the US military during World War I to gain US citizenship. After the war Simon moved to Colorado, worked for the railroad and saved his money so he could eventually start his own business. In 1922 he moved to a small suburb of Chicago known as Andersonville, using the money he had saved to open a small café.

One day two gentlemen reportedly came in and ordered coffee. One then added whiskey to it, slid it over to Simon, and told him to try it. Simon did and exclaimed that it was "some very good whiskey!"

The bootleggers (rumored to be members of Al Capone's gang) told Simon they could get him a regular supply and put the word out that he was to be left alone. He accepted, and as word got out that whiskey was available in Simon's cafe his business grew rapidly. By 1926 he needed to expand the size of his "bar," and he purchased the building where the bar remains today.

Initially he merely sold the laced coffee, but he quickly realized it would be more profitable to sell the whiskey alone. So in the mid-1920s he opened a speakeasy below the café, calling it the N. N. Club (reportedly standing for the No Name Club) and painting the door green.

1933 marked the end of Prohibition and the closing of illicit speakeasies. It also enabled Simon to go public (so to speak) with his bar. He moved from the basement to the café above, modeling it after the cruise ship Normandy (at the time the most expensive ever built), with a 60-foot-long mahogany bar, images of the ship etched into the glass above the registers and portholes in the bar-back.

Simon also started a community bank of sorts, cashing the paychecks of his patrons every Friday (over $14,000 worth in 1934 dollars). The "bank" is under the stairs to the top stories of the building and still retains all of Simon's security features, like bullet-proof glass and a heavy steel door.

TODAY

Today Simon's Tavern continues to operate at the same location and with much of the same décor. Current owner and operator Scott Martin bought the bar from Simon's son, Roy, and has continued to keep the bar's rich traditions in place. As one example, every year Scott makes over 2,000 gallons of traditional Swedish glogg—a hot, spiced wine—serving it from Thanksgiving through the end of winter.

The food menu is limited to small, frozen, oven-baked pizza. It's bar food at its worst, but honestly, who cares about the food with all of the other rich history in this place?

Another of the artifacts left from Lumberg's tenure is a huge hand-painted canvas mural on the wall opposite the bar. The mural, painted by Lumberg's friend and fellow Swede, Sig Olson, depicts what was known as the Deer Hunter's Ball, a celebration held in a distant cabin on the last weekend of deer hunting season every year. The mural took Olson six years to paint and

was presented to Lumberg in 1956. Look for five hidden animals in the painting, and if you find them all, drinks are on the house all night (and you get to wear the Viking helmet). Also, ask the bartender about the ghost that haunts Simon's and the revenge she exacted on the painting.

THE DRINKS

Almost every Swedish family has their own, closely guarded secret recipe for glogg, and Simon's is no different (Scott wouldn't reveal his recipe to us no matter how hard we tried).

Because glogg is a hot holiday drink, Scott doesn't serve it all year. Instead he has come up with a frozen glogg recipe that is available via a frozen margarita machine for the warmer months. Because we visited in July that's what we had to try,

and try it we did. Essentially it is a spiced-wine slushy and actually very good. If you visit after Thanksgiving but before the end of winter, definitely try the real glogg.

Another drink to try is Aquavit, a popular Scandinavian spirit that takes its name from the Latin words "aqua vitae," meaning water of life. It is a potato-based spirit like vodka, but flavored slightly with caraway, cardamom, cumin, anise, and fennel (but caraway is by far the dominant flavor). The particular brand of Aquavit they serve is Linie, made in Norway. Definitely try a shot, yelling "skol!" before you drink.

NEARBY DISTRACTIONS

Brew Camp
2039 W. Belle Plaine Ave. Chicago, IL 60618 (773) 857-2400 (Monday-Friday 12pm-8pm, Saturday-Sunday 10am-8pm).

Have a little time and want to learn about home brewing or wine making? At Brew Camp, just two miles away from Simon's, you can take an hour-and-a-half class on either of these subjects or even submit your own recipe and have it prepared. Class times vary, so check their website or give them a call.

Swedish American Museum
5211 N. Clark St. Chicago, IL 60640 (773) 728-8111 (Monday-Friday 10 am-4 pm, Saturday-Sunday 11 am-4pm).

Located directly across the street from Simon's Tavern is this non-profit museum and cultural center. Featuring both permanent and special exhibits, it celebrates Swedish American culture of Chicago and is a worthwhile visit to better understand the history of Swedish immigrants and therefore the history of Simon's Tavern and its founder.

Graceland Cemetery
4001 North Clark St. Chicago, IL 60613 (773) 525-1105.

A walkable 1.3 miles from Simon's Tavern, Graceland Cemetery has drawn admirers to its highly regarded architecture, art, and horticulture since opening in 1860. With world-famous monuments reminiscent of ancient Egyptian grandeur, this is a Chicago must-stop for any architectural admirer.

THE ORIGINAL MOTHER'S
CHICAGO, IL

26 West Division St.
Chicago, IL 60610
(312) 642-7251
http://www.originalmothers.com
http://youtu.be/s96r5Jluz_M

Food: No
Live Music: Sometimes, typically a DJ
Hours: Sunday—Friday 8pm-4am, Saturday 8pm-5am
Type of Bar: Nightclub
What to Drink: Schlitz, Adios Motherfucker (AMF)
Why You Should Go: One of the first venues for Cream, the Velvet Underground and other milestone bands.

This throwback to the early era of punk rock has been an incubator for different styles of music that have influenced dozens of famous musicians. It's also practically a Chicago institution, and a spot where you're sure to see visiting celebrities from any number of fields, including sports and music.

THE HISTORY

Mother's opened in 1968 and has been a Chicago favorite ever since. Starting in the 1970's it was and still to this day is THE singles club in the Rush and Division district (and arguably in the city of Chicago). However it wasn't the only club of its kind to open in that area. Not too far away was the famed Whiskey a Go Go, which opened in 1958 and then spread throughout the country.

At its roots, Mother's origin was about live music, and it hosted many of the bands we think of today as icons. At the time the bands were small or underground acts, which makes it even more significant, as Mother's gave them a fairly sizable venue in which to play.

Some of the more notable bands it hosted included Andy Warhol's Velvet Underground, Eric Clapton and Cream, The Mekons, and, of course, Chicago. What's amazing about this list is all of these bands are cited as some of the most influential bands and musicians ever, influencing many more to come after them.

In the late 1970s and early 1980s, after a brief but depressing disco period, Mother's became the source for the genre known as "house music," an electronic synthesized style invented by resident DJs. As before, the influence of what started at Mother's went on to create further styles of dance and hip-hop music, and formed the talent of contemporary artists like Madonna, Janet Jackson and Bjork.

Throughout its history, Mother's became known for both its architectural style—a kind of industrial war zone effect—and its consistent focus on music and changing trends. Though only 34 years young, Mother's has a significant place in the history of bars in the US.

TODAY

Today Mother's tradition of outstanding house music, live bands, and a karaoke setup that would satisfy any karaoke fiend is still firmly grounded and keeps the place crowded virtually every night. In addition to its continued prolific music scene, it plays host to some of the best and most popular events around

Chicago, including Elvis Fest, the Indie Incubator Film Fest, and the always popular Mardi Gras party.

When you enter the front door and head downstairs, you are welcomed into what can only be described as a cavernous venue. The place has three bars and two VIP lounges that regularly host an ensemble of local and national celebrities as well as locals and visitors. Make time to walk the dance floor and stage if you can, remembering that this is where Clapton came into his own in 1969 and 1970.

The décor can only be described as inspired; it is truly unique and has been left alone for the last 40 years (though we're told they moved the statuary around somewhat). It probably never goes out of style because it is pretty much its own style.

One of Mother's biggest claims to fame is the 1980s "Brat Pack" movie "About Last Night." In this romantic comedy, viewers follow Rob Lowe and Demi Moore, who are veterans of the Chicago singles scene, on their journey to become comfortable with commitment and with each other. It is a mildly funny movie that gives viewers some insight into 1980s Chicago.

Significant for Mother's is that the original play the movie was based on featured the bar as a character itself. In fact it was set at Mother's, that's how well-known this place was in the area. Before you go, give the movie a try, just to catch the décor and bars that you'll see when you arrive.

THE DRINKS

Mother's loves its drink specials. In fact, when we arrived they were featuring "Recession Buster Monday," with inexpensive beer and well drinks. And by inexpensive we mean about half the cost of anywhere else in the Rush and Division area: $3 domestic bottles, $3 house shots, $4 import bottles, and $7 Long Islands and other well drinks.

To make this a true experience, try a mixed drink typically found at nightclubs, the Adios Motherfucker. Sip it, and then hand it off to the 21-year-old hipster next to you. Then order a Schlitz and imagine Clapton tearing it up onstage.

NEARBY DISTRACTIONS

Rush and Division

The area Mother's resides in is known as Rush and Division, an area known for its assortment of dining, drinking, nightlife and entertainment. Featuring historic bars like The Lodge Tavern, She-nannigans and Mother's Too, to name just a few, a trip to Mother's isn't complete without visiting at least one of the legendary surrounding bars.

Gibson's

1028 North Rush Street, Chicago, IL 60611 (866) 442-7664 (open every day, lunch 11am-3pm, dinner 3pm-12am).

In the mood for steak? Then Gibson's is the place for you. Considered one of the top two places for steak in all of Chicago, it is less than a quarter mile from Mother's. Stop here for an outstanding steak dinner before you head out to Rush and Division for a night of drinking. If you're a fan of the television show, The League, you'll immediately recognize the outside sign.

Newberry Library & Washington Square Park (aka Bughouse Square)

60 West Walton St. Chicago, IL 60610 (312) 943-9090 (operating hours vary, check website or call).

Less than a half mile from Mother's, this world-renowned independent research library has free exhibitions, speaking events, and a rare and vast collection of non-circulated works. Directly across the street is Washington Square Park, which was donated to the city in 1842 and designated as a place of assembly and discussion.

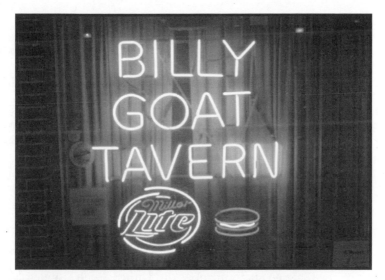

 # THE BILLY GOAT TAVERN

CHICAGO, IL

430 N. Michigan Ave. at Lower Level
Chicago, IL 60611
(312) 222-1525
http://www.billygoattavern.com
http://youtu.be/BIW47KJLi-Q

Food: Yes
Live Music: No
Hours: Monday—Friday 6am-2am,
Saturday 10am-2am, Sunday 11am-2am
Type of Bar: Pub
What to Drink: Schlitz
Why You Should Go: History of Chicago,
Saturday Night Live, Curse of the Billy Goat.

If you blink, you'll miss it. It's a sign on Michigan Avenue, a stone's throw from the river flanked by the Tribune Towers and cluttered with foot traffic. The sign is over a set of stairs that recede into darkness. The sign says "World Famous Billy Goat Tavern & Grill, Lower Level." Follow these stairs down and you've found it: the entrance to some of the most colorful stories and bar lore in the United States at the world-famous Billy Goat Tavern.

THE HISTORY

The original Billy Goat Tavern was located across the street from the Chicago stadium, now the United Center, and was founded in 1934 by Greek immigrant William "Billy Goat" Sianis. When he originally purchased the place it was called the Lincoln Tavern, and Sianis paid the sale price in full with a $205 check that bounced (he later paid for it in full with the profits from his first weekend's sales).

The name of the tavern was changed when a goat fell off a passing truck and wandered inside. William decided to adopt the goat, naming it Murphy, and then grew a goatee and took the nickname "Billy Goat." Finally, he decided to change the name of the bar from the Lincoln Tavern to the Billy Goat Tavern.

Billy Goat Sianis was a true master of PR and used his skill to keep the bar packed and constantly in the public eye. In 1944 the Republican Convention was being held in Chicago, and with it came numerous media trucks. The trucks blocked the front of his bar and restaurant, so Billy posted signs stating "No

Republicans Allowed," which of course packed the place with hundreds of Republicans and got Sianis tons of great press.

Another (perhaps the most notorious) publicity stunt occurred during the 1945 World Series. The Cubs were playing game four and were cruising to victory. Billy tried to bring his goat in to watch the game, but was denied because patrons said the goat stunk. He left dejected, and when the Cubs ended up losing the last two games, Sianis sent a telegram saying, "Who stinks now?"

This made the paper, and when a reporter asked if he cursed them, he said he did, and The Curse of the Billy Goat began.

In 1964 Billy Goat moved his tavern to its present subterranean location at 430 N. Michigan Avenue and slowly expanded to nine locations, with more on the way. His move to Michigan Ave. put the Billy Goat right in the center of the many Chicago-based newspapers and turned it into a regular spot for reporters.

On October 22, 1970, William Sianis passed away at the St. Clair Hotel where he had made his home. He passed the bar on to his nephew, Sam Sianis, who currently owns and operates it with his wife and six children.

TODAY

Today the Tavern is considered a Chicago tourist landmark and is visited by hundreds of locals, world travelers, politicians and actors on a daily basis. Some of the more notable guests include President George W. Bush, President Bill Clinton, Jay Leno, Bill Murray, John Belushi, and Frank Sinatra. Almost all of them have their picture on the wall posing with either William or Sam.

The place has a long bar that takes up most of one side of the restaurant, red-and-white checkered tablecloths, and walls filled with pictures of the many celebrities that have stopped in. There are also newspaper articles written by the many regular columnists and reporters, a whole wall dedicated to the "Billy Goat" himself, and TVs that are constantly showing Chicago sports teams.

In the center of the room is a U-shaped counter, and behind that is a long, flat grill, on which meat, topped with cheese, is heard sizzling just below the sound of shouting from the people working the grill.

The place feels busy and even a little cramped, but it also feels like a good old-fashioned family restaurant, not the icon it is. Here you won't find the sterile feeling of the chain restaurants on Michigan Ave. above you. This is a place to enjoy the food and the characters working the grill and bar.

And if you're a Saturday Night Live fan, the grill may seem a bit familiar to you, but there's a good reason why. In the 1970s when the place was busy, Sam (who has an oatmeal-thick Greek accent) rushed from customer to customer taking and calling out orders. It sounded something like this:

"Who's next!?! WHO'S NEXT!?!"

"Don't look at menu, look at ME! I order for you—DOU-BLECHEEZ!"

"No! DOUBLECHEEZ!!!!"

"It's Friday, doublecheez for everybody! It's payday! Triplecheez for the big guy!"

"No fries—CHEEPS!"

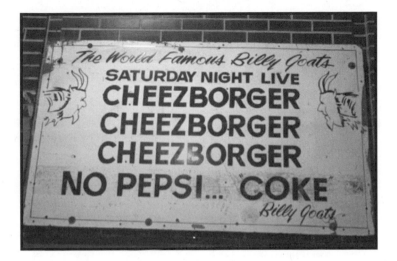

"No Pepsi–COKE!"

This was all immortalized in 1978 when Saturday Night Live aired a skit called Olympia Café, starring John Belushi, Bill Murray, Dan Aykroyd, and Loraine Newman. John Belushi and Bill Murray knew of the Billy Goat from their days at Second City, a nearby comedy sketch theater. Look up the video on YouTube BEFORE you get here.

THE FOOD

Speaking of Cheezeborgers, the food at the Billy Goat is simple, quick, and consists mainly of those world-famous burgers, which by themselves are worth coming in for.

The beef used in the patties is ground and prepared fresh by the family. You can get single, double, or triple cheese, with all the fixings you could possibly want. Holding true to their roots, the location on Lower Michigan Avenue still does not serve Pepsi or fries (although we were told that some of the other locations have started to serve fries due to popular demand). Either way, the burgers are great, the atmosphere is fantastic, and the trip to grab a bite to eat, watch some Chicago sports, and listen to the interaction of the cooks is well worth the journey.

THE DRINKS

Billy Goat doesn't carry many of the popular brands on tap—they never have. Coors Light and Budweiser fans will have to go elsewhere. But they've had a Schlitz account forever and still pour it fresh from the tap all day long. Luckily, Schlitz is no longer rotgut; they've gone back to their original recipe that made them so famous years ago. It's a good beer, especially with a burger and good conversation.

NEARBY DISTRACTIONS

Chicago Tribune Building
435 N Michigan Ave #1, Chicago, IL 60611 (312) 222-3994 (operating hours vary; call ahead).

Located directly across the street from the stairs that take you down to The Billy Goat is Tribune Tower. Home of the Chicago Tribune Newspaper, this neo-Gothic-themed building was completed in 1925 after a worldwide architecture competition in 1922. The lobby has a relief map of the United States made from shredded US currency, and it still houses offices for Chicago Tribune writers, whose predecessors were the original regulars at the legendary Billy Goat. Take a minute on your way down to or up from the Billy Goat to appreciate an outstanding example of Chicago's unique skyline.

Giordano's
130 E Randolph Drive, Chicago, IL 60601 (312) 616-1200 (Daily 11am-11pm).

No trip to Chicago is complete without some deep dish pizza, and few places do it better than Giordano's. Originally opened in 1974 by Italy born Efren and Joesph Boglio, and only a half mile from the Billy Goat, the pizza is worth the walk and the wait. Usually a busy place, so expect a wait during prime dining times. Order your pizza before you are seated to get your pie a little quicker.

Navy Pier
600 E Grand Ave., Chicago, IL 60611 (Hours vary with season and events).

Less than a mile from The Billy Goat is Chicago's Navy Pier. Featuring an amusement park, Landshark Beer Garden, regularly scheduled fireworks, seasonal events and a multitude of stage shows, the Navy Pier has something for just about everyone. Check their schedule of events at navypier.com before you go.

GREEN DOOR TAVERN

CHICAGO, IL

678 N. Orleans St.
Chicago, IL 60654
(312) 664-5496
http://www.greendoorchicago.com
http://youtu.be/NqK4ywT1s08

Food: Yes
Live Music: Yes
Hours: Monday—Friday 11:30am-2am,
Saturday 11:30am-3am, Sunday 12pm-9pm
Type of Bar: Pub
What to Drink: French 75
Why You Should Go: Original Chicago speakeasy, last
wooden structure built in downtown Chicago.

There are many, many pubs and taverns in America that lay claim to being a speakeasy during Prohibition, but few are documented, and fewer still retained the speakeasy portion after 1933. The Green Door Tavern in Chicago, though, is one of those few. With great food, a great bar staff and atmosphere and (oh yeah) a legitimate speakeasy downstairs, this is a must-see if you're anywhere within a hundred miles.

THE HISTORY

Immediately following the Great Chicago fire of 1871, James McCole, an area engineer, built a two-story wooden building and a detached cottage on a piece of property located close to downtown Chicago. He initially rented the property to a grocer, Lawrence P. Ek, as a combination grocery store and apartment.

Shortly afterwards Chicago passed a law prohibiting any commercial wooden structures in the Central Business District. McCole's building, however, was grandfathered in, making the building not only one of the few wooden-framed structures built in the district after the fire, but also the last freestanding wooden structure in downtown Chicago.

In 1921 an Italian restaurant called The Heron Orleans replaced the grocery store. Soon after opening the owner passed away, and so his kids did like any entrepreneurs of the time would do: they opened a speakeasy downstairs.

During Prohibition, a green door on the street meant there was a speakeasy located on the other side. Opening to the street

below the Heron Orleans was the green door leading downstairs (the fixture for which the Green Door Tavern gets its name).

Their alcohol was supplied by the North Side Gang and more specifically by Irish-American mobster and bootlegger Dean O'Banion. This would have made the Green Door and its suppliers an enemy of the more notorious Al Capone (who had O'Banion killed in 1924).

TODAY

Today the Green Door Tavern continues to be the last freestanding wooden structure in downtown Chicago, and is described by manager and co-owner Jeff Lynch as "a neighborhood watering hole that serves great food and outstanding drinks." A statement we wholeheartedly agree with.

The exterior has changed very little since its building and it still maintains that very classic 1920s persona. Upon entering through the heavy green, crooked door, visitors are greeted by a bar interior decorated in the manner most chain restaurants try to copy. The bar is comfortable, dripping with varnished wood and personality. It's a place you feel at home in, with great food, powerful and well-crafted drinks, and one of the coolest original speakeasies in the entire country found just downstairs (rented for private parties and events).

Another unique aspect of the Green Door Tavern is the leaning or "racking" of the building. If you don't notice the lean from the outside, you definitely will when you come through the front door, which not only swings in but swings up as well. It can also be seen when compared to the building next door, or in the entrance to the office below the bar.

The racking is a common occurrence of wooden buildings after settling over the years. However, as disconcerting as it might seem, the building is as solid as can be, and there's no danger of impending collapse.

THE FOOD

The food at this place is simply outstanding. They're known for their chili and burgers, but when we visited we tried the corned beef sandwich, which we promptly fell in love with. The corned beef is slowly baked (not boiled) for hours, making it moist and melt-in-your-mouth tender. Combined with some seasoned, fresh-cut French fries and a dill pickle spear, and you've one of the best meals available downtown.

THE DRINKS

There really isn't a wrong drink to order here—as long as it's a classic cocktail, which they excel at making.

One to try is the French 75, a Prohibition-era cocktail invented in 1915 and named for the French 75 MM howitzer (what it's supposed to kick like). It's made with gin, simple syrup, sweet and sour, and then topped with champagne. It is much sourer than it might sound, and it's really refreshing on a hot, humid Chicago day.

http://youtu.be/kgc8w76Bcl4

NEARBY DISTRACTIONS

Chicago Brew Bus

(773) 340-2739 (Fri-Sun, times vary; check their website or call, private tours available).

If you're into craft beers and pub food and want to try a few of Chicago's best in a short period, then the Chicago Brew Bus tour may be just the thing for you. Starting at the Goose Island Brewery (less than two miles from the Green Door) the tour takes you to at least three local breweries with approximately one hour at each. It includes free samples at every stop, and they'll even store and chill any growler you decide to purchase. A great way to spend an afternoon after having lunch at the Green Door.

Willis Tower (Formerly Sears Tower)

233 South Wacker Drive Chicago, IL 60606 (312) 875-9696 (operating hours vary by season; visit the website or call for more information).

Formerly known as the Sears Tower, a name most refuse to relinquish, it's the most iconic and recognizable skyscraper in the Chicago skyline. Just over a mile from the Green Door, no visit to Chicago is complete without at least getting close enough to stare up at this impressive example of American ingenuity. For the complete experience, head up to the Skydeck to get an experience of a lifetime while standing in a clear box extended out from the tower.

HALA KAHIKI

CHICAGO, IL

2834 North River Road
River Grove, IL 60171
(708) 456-3222
http://www.hala-kahiki.com
http://youtu.be/xpcY_vQk2X4

Food: No
Live Music: No
Hours: Monday—Tuesday 7pm-2am, Wednesday—Friday, Sunday 4pm-2am, Saturday 4pm-3am
Type of Bar: Tiki bar
What to Drink: Scorpion Bowl, Lava Bowl, Puffer Fish
Why You Should Go: Original Tiki bar from early '60s, huge collection of period furniture and art, all booze no food.

Though there have been many different and passion-ate arguments over what makes a vintage Tiki bar, one thing that has always been a common characteristic is its abil-ity to whisk you away to a far-off tropical paradise. Outside of Chicago that's exactly what you'll find at the Hala Kahiki.

THE HISTORY

Originally opened in 1963 by Rose and Stanley Sacharski, Hala Kahiki started life as the Lucky Start. Stanley was a mor-tician in his family's mortuary business, but after a falling out with his family, he decided to do something different with his life, and thus opened the bar.

The original bar didn't have a tropical theme. In fact that didn't happen until Stanley was making some renovations and wanted to hide the poor condition of the walls. So he hung some bamboo siding purchased from Sears and Roebuck, mainly because it was cheap. But customers saw the change and asked if the bar was turning into a Tiki bar (which were popular at the time), and the idea snowballed from there.

The bar quickly grew in popularity, and so they moved it to a larger venue in River Grove, Illinois. The location was pre-viously a trucker bar called the Glasshouse (originally an old Greenhouse). It still resides there today, only a short cab ride from Chicago's O'Hare airport.

The name was changed to Hala Kahiki after Stanley's son, Sonny, was reading a Dennis the Menace comic titled "Dennis the Menace Goes to Hawai'i." In the comic Hala Kahiki was mentioned and after a bit of investigation he found that Hala Kahiki is a pineapple plantation in Hawai'i (it actually means, "House of Pineapple"), and so the Sacharski's decided it was the perfect name for their new Tiki bar.

TODAY

Upon entering you find yourself in a tropical paradise located in the middle of the busy Chicago Metro area. The décor is all original and features the largest collection of original Witco art-work of any Tiki bar in the US. Witco was one of the most pop-ular designers of South Sea décor during the 1960s and 1970s. Witco was so popular, in fact, that Elvis commissioned them to design and decorate the Jungle Room in Graceland.

Much of the rest of the décor is standard Tiki—outrigger canoes on the ceiling, bamboo furniture and fixtures, and tapa cloth and netting on the walls.

There are Tikis strewn about as well, especially on the outside patio, a lush oasis complete with tropical plants, fountain and pond. This place is the perfect escape at night when the torches are lit and Hawaiian music is piped in through the speakers.

THE DRINKS

The bar features over 125 drinks, and while we asked to try them all (we were told no), we were lucky enough to try a handful of them and came up with some favorites.

The first is the Chi Chi, a different spin on the piña colada and made with vodka instead of rum. Because of the more neutral taste of the vodka, the coconut and cream become the main focus of the drink and not the rum.

We were also pretty impressed with their Scorpion Bowl, which they wouldn't give us the recipe to. While expecting something somewhat sweet like the drink at other Tiki bars, we were really surprised at the sharp kick of the spirits.

Our final recommendation is the Puffer Fish, a martini made with pineapple vodka, pineapple juice, and some secret ingredients.

http://youtu.be/i7PLndpeIC4

NEARBY DISTRACTIONS

Ernest Hemingway Foundation Oak Park
200 North Park Avenue, Oak Park, IL 60302 (708) 445-3071
(Sunday-Friday 1 pm-5 pm, Saturday 10 am-5 pm).

About five miles from the Hala Kahiki is Ernest Hemingway's birthplace. Born on the second story of this Queen Anne-style house on July 21st, 1899, Ernest spent the first six years of his life here. A short walk away is the Ernest Hemingway Museum, which is housed in the Oak Park Arts Center. Offering guided tours throughout the day a visit here is well worth the trip to get a glimpse into the life and works of arguably the most influential author of the 20th century.

Maywood Park Racetrack

8600 West North Avenue, Melrose Park, IL 60160 (708) 343-4800 (Open year-round with varying live racing days).

Featuring live harness racing since 1932, this is considered the US's fastest harness race track. Stop in to watch a live race, place a small wager to make things a little more interesting, and enjoy a reprieve from Chicago's hustle and bustle.

Melrose Park Indoor Grand Prix

2225 W. North Ave. Melrose Park, IL 60160 (708) 343-7223 (Hours vary by season; check website or call).

Feel like getting in touch with the Al Unser in you? If so, head to Melrose Park Indoor Grand Prix which is only 2.4 miles from Hala Kahiki. Featuring quick nine-horsepower carts and an indoor track for "all season fun," this place is sure to bring out the kid in everyone.

OTHER NOTABLE AREA BARS

Schaller's Pump

3714 South Halsted Street Chicago, IL 60609 (773) 376-6332 (Monday-Friday 11am-2am, Saturday 4pm-3am).

Serving Chicago's Bridgeport neighborhood for over 125 years, this place is awash in Chicago history. Located close to both the old and new Comiskey and across the street from the district's Democrat Party Headquarters, the saloon serves as a hangout for both White Sox fans and the politically connected (including five of the city's mayors, who heralded from Bridgeport). It was, like so many others, a speakeasy during Prohibition, and they're happy to point out the peephole used to discern the customers from the fuzz.

The Berghoff

17 West Adams Street Chicago, IL 60603 (312) 408-0200 (Monday-Friday 11am-9pm, Saturday 11:30am-9pm).

This Chicago institution was founded in 1898 by German immigrant Herman Joseph Berghoff, who wanted to bring a piece of home to the many other German immigrants flooding Chicago at the time. They serve authentic German cuisine and, of course, beer—lots of it. Berghoff made his own lager, and apparently his brewery was pretty popular. His beer was so popular, in fact, that during Prohibition when he actually did go dry and made near beer, he still sold gallons of it to locals.

Southport Lanes

3325 North Southport Avenue Chicago, IL 60657 (773) 472-6600 (Monday-Friday 12pm-2am, Saturday 12pm-3am, Sunday 12pm-1am).

Yep, we're talking about a bowling alley. But one with history and notoriety. This place was originally built by Schlitz in 1922—which doesn't really make sense if you think about it. In any case, all it could serve was Schlitz, but it apparently did well. However, that wasn't always the case. Once Schlitz sold the bar the new owners had a tough time making ends meet. So, they put prostitutes on the menu and ran a brothel out of the top floors. Being discreet folks, they advertised by the murals on the walls depicting naked nymphs and other erotica.

AUSTIN

Austin, Texas, is one of the most dynamic cities in the United States. The mix of politics, western history and of course the state's largest university creates a lively and sometimes eccentric environment.

Austin is known as an entertainment destination. From concerts to sporting events, the city seems to have something to offer everyone. That includes those looking to quench their thirst. Most famous is the downtown area where 4th and 6th Streets overflow with bars and nightclubs. Most of these are trendy music venues for the Austin "weird" crowd: hipsters, college students and young professionals.

We don't want to have anything to do with this area. The bars change often, the scene is more in tune with what sells at the moment and less about authenticity. Instead, we want to get off these streets and look at other places at which hoist a cold one.

The legacy of Austin's drinking history is intertwined with the huge influx of German settlers coming into the region. In the 1830s a German immigrant wrote a letter to a friend back in Germany that described the beauty and wealth of Texas. The letter was subsequently published in the town's paper and ended up being quite influential in drawing more immigrants to the area.

The German influence can easily be seen in the local architecture (more a Bavarian influence than Mexican or Spanish), in the history of brewing (lagers over other types of beer), and even in the last names of many of the oldest families.

The influence was also substantial on the bar history of the town, and at least two of our picks for Austin Bucket List Bars™ reflect that legacy.

TRANSPORTATION: Yellow Cab Austin Taxi Service (512) 452-9999 (Monday-Sunday 24hrs). North Austin Taxi Services LLC (512) 704-9999 (Monday-Sunday 24hrs).

SCHOLZ GARTEN

AUSTIN, TX

1607 San Jacinto Boulevard
Austin, TX 78701
(512) 474-1958
http://www.scholzgarten.net
http://youtu.be/GvROvzMUNoI

Food: Yes
Live Music: Yes
Hours: Monday—Sunday 11am-12am
Type of Bar: Beer Garden
What to Drink: Beer. Any kind.
Why You Should Go: One of the oldest bars in the United
States, great tradition and history, German immigrants,
experience the thrill of UT football game night.

Surrounded by parking garages and just a few short blocks away from the legendary Darrell K. Royal-Texas Memorial Stadium sits the nondescript brick building that is actually Austin's most historic bar. When confronted with lederhosen, bratwurst and polka, you'll know you've arrived at the oldest beer garden in the county.

THE HISTORY

Scholz Garten was founded in 1866 by August Scholz, a German immigrant and confederate veteran. Originally purchased in 1862 from Sam Norville for the sum of $2400, the property contained a boarding house above which August eventually built his bar and café. Scholz Garten quickly became a popular meeting and hangout location for Austin's German population. Eventually August converted the downstairs to a bar as well and installed a traditional Bavarian beer garden—an outdoor sitting area where bands play and beer flows like water.

After August's death in 1891, his stepson, Theodor Reisner, took over the operation of the Garten until selling the establishment to the Lemp Brewery, makers of Falstaff Beer, in 1893. That year just so happened to be the same year the University of Texas football team went undefeated, and thanks to the Garten's geographic location, only two blocks from the stadium, it quickly became THE place to celebrate the school's wins (a tradition that continues to this day).

The bar was again sold in 1908 to the German singing club

"The Austin Saengerrunde," who still own the property today though the bar and restaurant are leased.

And as it did for so many establishments across the nation the 18th Amendment had a dramatic effect on Scholz Garten. To survive, they created a non-alcoholic brew called Bone Dry Beer and increased the focus on their food, featuring both German and Texas favorites, a tradition that continues today.

TODAY

Today Scholz Garten is well known for being exactly the same as it's always been, and in a time of constant changes, updates, and renovations, that's a unique characteristic. Little is different about the place after over 100 years of operation. As a matter of fact, in 1962 when then operator Bob Bales decided to add

air conditioning, he claimed he was almost run out of town by unhappy patrons. Needless to say, the regulars like the Garten and want it left just the way it is.

Scholz Garten has become a rite of passage for University of Texas students and fans, an iconic location to celebrate UT victories and to mourn their losses. It's also a staple in Austin's bar scene and continues to be a local favorite.

Also, because of its geographic location and historic importance, Scholz Garten has had more than its fair share of politicians stop in for a cold beer, bite to eat, and a friendly debate or two. Notable visitors include almost all of Texas's governors (the Democrats, anyway), Bill Clinton, Al Gore, and more than a handful of Texas state representatives. The outdoor Garten attracts the more liberal politicians, while the indoor area tends to attract the conservatives (makes one wonder where the independents go).

When you visit you might hear a mysterious sound often heard while standing around the outdoor beer garden. It's an occasional rumble and boom, kind of like rolling thunder, but heard on both stormy and clear days. Its source is known by only a few: it's the Scholz' bowling alley (now you know too).

The bowling alley is located on opposite side of the north wall lining the beer garden. It was built by the Lemp Brewing Company sometime around 1893 and is still in operation today. If you ask around, find the right person and beg for admission (it is a private club) you too could enjoy a few rounds of bowling with a nice cold pitcher, just feet away from the historic beer garden.

THE FOOD

The most obvious choice is going to be the more traditional stuff. Brats and beer go together like, well, brats and beer. This is especially true at a beer garden. Order a bratwurst, sauerkraut, hard roll and mustard, and you can't go wrong.

They're also really well known for their barbecue, especially the Texas specialty: the brisket. They let us watch them preparing it, and we were drooling in no time. Get a plate of it and sit outside to listen to some traditional music. Give their four meat BBQ plate a try for a little of everything, and wash it down with an Austin Beerworks Pearl Snap Pilsner. Either way you go, you really can't go wrong.

THE DRINKS

While they used to only serve beer, they now feature a full bar and can make just about anything you might want. Though it's tempting to order Jaegermeister or maybe schnapps, you need to go with beer; after all, it is a beer garden.

They serve an immense amount of beer here, especially during a UT football game. And while we're typically not fans of the common American lagers and pilsners, it would actually be fitting to order it here. So take your pick, a Bud, Coors or Miller product outside in the garden would make for a great day (or night).

NEARBY DISTRACTIONS

Texas State History Museum
www.thestoryoftexas.com
1800 N. Congress Ave. Austin, TX 78701 (512) 936-4639
(Monday-Saturday 9am-6pm, Sunday 12pm-6pm).

Located less than a half mile from Scholz is the Texas State History Museum. Featuring three floors of interactive exhibits, a special effects show and Austin's only IMAX theatre, it is truly a Texas-sized museum (about one of the largest and most colorful states in the nation). Be sure to check out their website, as they often have special exhibits and events.

Bobalu Cigar Co.
www.bobalu.com
509 E. 6th Street Austin, TX 78701 (888) 332-4427
(operating hours vary, check website or call ahead).

Only a mile from Scholz is Bobalu Cigar Company. Makers of their own line of cigars, they pride themselves on being the microbrewery of the cigar business, with the freshest, best tasting cigars and fairest prices you'll find. They even have experienced Cuban Cigar Rollers on site that you can watch via cameras as they roll some of the finest cigars in the country. So whether you're a cigar connoisseur, a beginner or somewhere in between, Bobalu is worth checking out.

Joe Jamail Field Texas Memorial Stadium
www.texassports.com
San Jacinto Boulevard Austin, TX 78712 (512) 471-7437
(games, events, and tour times vary. Trophy room is open
to the public Monday-Friday 8am-5pm).

Few college sports programs or stadiums are as storied as that
of the Texas Longhorns football program. Less than a mile from
Scholz (you can see it from the front door), the stadium is a
beacon in Austin. If you can swing going to a game it will be
an unforgettable experience, and if not, then go on their self-
guided tour, which ends in the trophy room containing their
multiple national titles and Heisman trophies.

SCOOT INN
AUSTIN, TX

1308 East 4th Street
Austin, TX 78702
(512) 524-1932
http://www.scoot-inn.com
http://youtu.be/aPzCazDjAmo

Food: No
Live Music: Yes
Hours: Monday—Sunday 6pm-2am
Type of Bar: Dive, Beer Garden
What to Drink: Local craft beer, shot of Jack Daniels
Why You Should Go: History of Austin, beer garden, live music.

Opened in 1871 the Scoot Inn, aka Red's Scoot Inn, claims the title of the longest continuously running saloon in central Texas. If only these walls could talk. Of course, we've a feeling some wouldn't want them to.

THE HISTORY

The Scoot Inn was originally built as a railroad saloon in 1871 and played host to a long list of thirsty train passengers, railroad workers, bankers, outlaws, ranch hands, pioneers, travelers, and of course ladies of the night. From its opening in 1871 until around 1940 the place went through a long succession of own-ers, made a few changes, but refused to stop serving. Legend has it that the saloon has *never* closed its doors, even operating through Prohibition, faithfully serving locals and travelers alike.

In 1940 Scoot Ivy and his buddy Red bought the bar and named it Red's Scoot Inn. They served many of the same custom-ers as those served 70 years before: warehouse workers, railroad workers, travelers, and locals (not to mention themselves; rumor has it Red and Scoot were themselves big drinkers and sometime finished multiple cases in a day). The place got quite the reputa-tion during their tenure when most considered it the bar to be avoided in Austin through the 1970s. They owned, operated, and drank at the bar until 1980 when they both passed away.

The bar continued to operate, but it was a bit of a rough spell for a while until Vera Sandoval took ownership in 1997. Vera and her mother immediately set about cleaning up the place's image and attracting a new and more refined crowd. They ran

the place until 2006, when the owners of The Longbranch Inn just up the street purchased the Scoot Inn. They continue the tradition started over 130 years ago.

TODAY

The current owners of the Scoot Inn remodeled and renovated the old saloon by putting up period wallpaper, building indoor and outdoor stages, and creating an outdoor beer garden and music venue. They also actively seek out both small and larger bands to play on a weekly basis, making the Scoot Inn a popular live music venue for Austin locals and visitors.

Another popular feature they introduced in the bar were skee-ball machines. Skee-ball is a cornerstone of Scoot Inn and is rapidly gaining popularity in bars across the nation. The saloon features year-round leagues and occasional nightly competitions, and the lanes are open for anyone to try. Nationwide leagues like SkeeNation and United Social Sports are also gaining strength and turning skee-ball into a national competitive sport.

The Scoot Inn is now a lively destination for many in Austin, and for many that travel to Austin. It features regular live music and is one of the many entertainment venues for SXSW (South by Southwest), Austin's premier music, movie and multimedia expo and conference held every spring (even hosting the Thrasher party during the event).

THE DRINKS

The Scoot Inn is a traditional beer-and-shot bar with a long list of local beers. If you do find yourself in this historic saloon, we highly recommend Austin Beerworks Peacemaker—an extra pale ale—or maybe a Pearl Snap—a German style pilsner. If you're not in the mood for beer, then considering the

rough-and-tumble past of this old saloon, a shot of whiskey is definitely called for (Jack Daniels, rocks, comes to mind).

NEARBY DISTRACTIONS

Juan In A Million
www.juaninamillion.com
2300 Cesar Chavez Street Austin TX 78702 (512) 472-3872
(Monday-Sunday 7am-3pm)

If the beer and live music at the Scoot Inn leaves your stomach rumbling, then drive or walk the one mile from the Scoot Inn to Juan in a Million, and take on the breakfast taco challenge. To win, all you have to do is eat more Don Juan breakfast tacos than the current record, which as of now stands at eight, and you'll get your picture on the Juan Wall of Fame. Good luck.

Live Oak Brewing
www.liveoakbrewing.com
3301 E 5th Street Austin, TX 78702 (512) 385-2299
(tours occur twice per month, check website or call
for information and reservations).

You can never go wrong with free beer, especially when it is good free beer. At Live Oak Brewing Company the beer is good and on tours it is free, at least a small amount anyway. Only two miles away, it is yet another opportunity to taste some of Austin's outstanding craft beer offerings.

THE TAVERN
AUSTIN, TX

922 West 12th St.
Austin, TX 78703
(512) 320-8377
http://www.tavernaustin.com
http://youtu.be/4OcauzoWuSQ

Food: Yes
Live Music: Yes
Hours: Monday—Tuesday 8am-12am,
Wednesday—Saturday 8am-2am, Sunday 8am-10pm
Type of Bar: Sports Bar
What to Drink: A Fireman's 4 Blonde (local beer)
Why You Need to Go: Oldest sports bar in Texas, speak-
easy and brothel through Prohibition, tons of local history.

This is one of those places that grandparents take their grandkids to. The Tavern is a staple of Austin city life, serving for almost a century now, that looks like a portal to Bavaria—fitting considering this is one of the premier beer joints in town.

THE HISTORY

A phrase you'll hear often around Austin is "You're never too far from 12th and Lamar." It's a reference to the Tavern, the oldest sports bar in Texas, located on the corner of 12th Street and Lamar Boulevard. It is one of Texas' oldest bars and has a colorful history that makes any trip worthwhile.

The building was originally built in 1916 by owner R. Niles Graham, who had planned to build a bar at the location since day one; he hired Hugo Kuehne, a first generation German

immigrant, to design and build the building. Hugo decided to model the building after a traditional German public house, but plans had to be "modified" after the 18th Amendment was passed. In true can-do, can-win and can-make-the-best-of-the-situation attitude, Graham decided to build a grocery store in the bar's place (or at least that is what he wanted everyone to believe).

Rumor has it that the establishment was a grocery by day and a speakeasy by night. After closing, the downstairs was turned into a popular speakeasy complete with booze and gambling, and the upstairs contained a prominent brothel—some of the employees of which are said to still be with the place!

Like so many old establishments across the country, the Tavern is rumored to be haunted. Most believe the ghost of a prostitute named Emily, and possibly her daughter, still reside in the building today. It is thought that they were killed during an altercation between two men sometime in the early 1940s, though there is no hard evidence to prove this story. People have witnessed TV channels changing for no reason, glasses and plates falling unexpectedly, footsteps in the halls when no one is around, tray tables falling and unexplained phone calls.

One particularly creepy incident occurred late one night when the manager was upstairs on the third floor for closing. With nobody in the building, the manager received a call from the gas station attendant across the street, who wanted to know if the place was still open. The manager replied no, and the attendant asked why there was someone standing in the window on the second floor. The manager went to investigate and found no one and nothing out of the ordinary, so he called the gas station attendant back, but the attendant still insisted that the lady was in the window looking right at him.

Haunted or not, we didn't see anything, but if you do happen to see Emily or her daughter, tell her we said hello and would love an interview.

As if almost admitting to the illegal activities the grocery store was moved in 1929, and an upscale restaurant took its place. And then finally when Prohibition ended in 1933, Graham got his wish and was able to start serving alcoholic beverages (legally, of course).

TODAY

Today the saying "You're never too far from 12th and Lamar" continues to be an Austenite favorite as does the Tavern. The bar is a common hangout for people from all walks of life, and due to the huge number of high-definition flat screens, it's also a favorite on game day.

When entering, try a seat at the bar, carved up from artistic vandals over the years (if you have a pen knife you're welcome to carve your name, too). Or if you're brave enough and the place is kind of empty, take your drink and dish up to the top floors and hang out with one of the ghosts that haunt the joint.

And when we say that the crowd is varied here, we're not kidding. From doctors to students, politicians to businessmen, the Tavern seems to have something for everyone.

THE FOOD

The Tavern serves up a large array of sports bar-type fare, including burgers, salads, soups and the like. One of the more interesting dishes (for sports bar grub) is the plate of White Wings.

The White Wings are traditional chicken wings wrapped in bacon and jalapenos and tossed in their special wing sauce. They're actually pretty spicy but really tasty—the combination of wing sauce and bacon is just right.

THE DRINKS

The Tavern features a full bar, so they can mix up just about anything you want. However, they pride themselves on their local and craft beers, many of which aren't available outside of Austin.

We recommend the Fireman's 4 Blonde, a local beer that goes really well with the White Wings (if you decide to have them). They will also be happy to serve the beer in one of their oversized souvenir steins. Word of advice, though: if you do go for the oversized stein, be sure to get a cab ride home. Those things are no joke!

NEARBY DISTRACTIONS

K1 Speed

www.k1speed.com

2500 McHale Court Austin, TX 78758 (512) 271-5475
(Monday-Thursday 12pm-10pm, Friday 11am-11pm,
Saturday 10am-11pm, Sunday 10am-7pm).

If you're in the mood for some head-to-head racing with your friends, then head out to K1 speed, about 10 miles from The Tavern, for some fun indoor go-kart racing. For the ultimate experience, call ahead and plan an adult-only event.

Texas State Capitol

www.tspb.state.tx.us

1100 Congress Avenue Austin, TX 78701 (512) 463-0063
(operating hours vary by building and event).

An extraordinary example of 19th-century architecture, the Texas Capitol is approximately 22 acres of grounds and monuments. Less than a mile from the Tavern, admission is free and self-guided tours are available.

OTHER NOTABLE AREA BARS

Deep Eddy Cabaret

2315 Lake Austin Boulevard Austin, TX 78703 (512) 472-0961 (Monday-Sunday 12pm-2am).

This staple of Austin is a quiet place, geared towards relaxing with a drink in your hand and talking to friends. The place actually started life as a grocery store and bait shop in the 1920s, but in 1951 they converted to a beer joint. If you want to escape the loud music and crowds at other places, this might be your bar of choice.

Mickey's Thirsty-I-Lounge

11806 North Lamar Boulevard Austin, TX 78753 (512) 836-9991 (Monday-Saturday 8am-12am, Sunday 12pm-12am).

There's no telling how old this dive bar is, though it's been said that it's the oldest beer bar north of the Colorado River. This means, of course, that Mickey's is a beer bar, i.e., no booze. However, for a small fee you can tote your own bottle in and they'll care for it while you relax. They are known to be a great place for karaoke, so if you're into belting your lungs out in front of drunken strangers this is the place. The crowd is rowdy and weird, so expect some funk.

SAN ANTONIO

San Antonio is the city that many think of when they think of Texas history. And of course they think of it for good reasons. After all, this is the city in which Santa Anna laid siege to the Alamo and killed James Bowie, Davie Crockett and a small outnumbered force from the Texian Army.

This is also the heart of cattle country, and in the 1800s it saw many of the most successful cattle barons in the West walk her streets. The most famous and successful of these was Richard King, founder of the King Ranch, one of the largest ranches in the world.

It was also the host to Texas' first brewery (like Austin, San Antonio had a huge German immigrant population) and number of old West saloons. The brewery and all but one of the saloons are gone now, but their legacy lives on.

And like most cities, San Antonio has a darker side. In the 1960s they became home to the Mexican Mafia, a ruthless organized street gang that ran the underworld of the city, including one of our Bucket List Bars™.

Luckily much of that has changed. San Antonio has been cleaned up, and many of the bad elements have been escorted out of the city. It's still home to a huge military population, with Army, Marine and Air Force personnel stationed close by. The crowd you'll find will be a combination of business people, a stream of tourists, and military personnel looking to blow off some steam.

TRANSPORTATION: Yellow Cab San Antonio (210) 222-2222 (Monday-Sunday 24hrs). San Antonio Taxi (210) 444-2222 (Monday-Sunday 24hrs). National Cab Company (210) 434-4444 (Monday-Sunday 24hrs).

THE ESQUIRE TAVERN

SAN ANTONIO, TX

155 East Commerce Street
San Antonio, TX 78205
(210) 222-2521
http://www.esquiretavern-sa.com
http://youtu.be/N7hRgloDxVY

Food: Yes
Live Music: No
Hours: Monday—Wednesday & Sunday 11am–12am,
Thursday—Saturday 11am–2am
Type of Bar: Saloon
What to Drink: The Mas Chingoni
Why You Should Go: Earliest post-Prohibition bar in San
Antonio, gangland bar in the 1970s-1990s.

itting on San Antonio's world-famous River Walk, The Esquire Tavern is one of the oldest bars in the state. With a history drenched in a notorious past, today The Esquire is a throwback to what it was during its time as San Antonio's premier watering hole.

THE HISTORY

The Esquire was opened on December 6, 1933, by the Georges, a local family who intended to quench the city's thirst after the failed Great Experiment (that is, Prohibition). As you can imagine, it opened to much fanfare after 14 years of government imposed "dryness." In fact, opening day saw a line that stretched for over a block.

The Georges were immigrants from Greece and were pursuing the American Dream when they opened their bar.

Originally they tried to open on Houston Street but were denied their request by the City. Instead they were given the rights to open a bar on Commerce Street, which is where the bar resides today. This turned out to be to their advantage because the location developed into a premier locale on San Antonio's famous River Walk.

From 1933 until the bar shut down in 2006, the Esquire's demographics ebbed and flowed with that of the city of San Antonio. From notorious gangsters of the 1930s (who used to purchase guns just down the road), middle class professionals, hipsters, and the notorious Mexican Mafia (who ran prostitution and drugs out of the bar), the Esquire has seen it all.

Speaking of the Mexican Mafia: located above the original bathrooms, which were originally placed in the back of the building, was a loft known as the VIP Room. The small room contained a bed, a sink, and for the right amount of money, a female companion. In short, the VIP room was the Esquire's "Champagne Room," or as is known in the masseuse realm, a place to obtain a "Happy Ending."

This was one of the products of the Mexican Mafia, a vicious gang of Latino street thugs that originated in San Antonio. From the late 1970s through early 2000s (when the bar finally closed), they used the Esquire to deal drugs and to run their prostitution ring. It was a rough place with a rough crowd. Nightly The Esquire saw stabbings, shootings and fights. There were metal detectors at the door and they even sold t-shirts that read, "I Survived The Esquire Tavern."

In 2006 the bar shut down and took a five-year hiatus. It had garnered a bad reputation and was known as a place to expect trouble. But then in 2008 local businessman Chris Hill purchased the troubled saloon with the goal of restoring it. He told a local newspaper, "The more I looked at it, the more I realized I didn't want someone to open a barbecue joint there. I mean, I can remember going there and having a great time. I thought it was important to downtown that there's one old original space left on the river."

When Hill purchased the bar it was badly dilapidated and in desperate need of renovations. After over a year remodeling, he brought the bar back to life in 2011 with a custom but vintage look that welcomes patrons just like it did in 1933.

TODAY

Today the Esquire has been renovated and displays its heritage through custom, vintage-looking décor. The furnishings are still some of the original (though restored), and the bar is still the longest one in Texas (more than 100 feet long). It also features an upscale, full-service kitchen with great burgers and some of the best fried pickles in all of Texas. But what really sets The Esquire apart from other establishments on the River Walk (besides its age) is its traditional approach to cocktails.

THE FOOD

We've heard rave reviews about their food. Their executive chef has blended regional cuisine and bar staples into a full menu of some great choices.

For an appetizer we had the fried pickles, which were just remarkable washed down with a cold beer (for some reason fried pickles always seem to hide the fact that they're about a thousand degrees until you bite into them, so be careful). The Bison Burger is supposed to be second to none, and even the bartenders

went on about it (and you know they're honest people).

THE DRINKS

The bartenders at The Esquire have mastered the lost art of professional bartending. Drinks, both traditional and house specialties, are made to exact specifications, giving patrons a consistent and true taste to their cocktails. As a matter of fact, some of the regulars told us that they sometimes feel guilty drinking their cocktails after watching the level of work and pride the bartenders put into them.

During our visit we were lucky enough to spend our time with The Esquire's former master barman and cocktail aficionado,

Jeret Pena, who just opened his own place, The Brooklynite. Besides being what some would consider a black belt in the art of barman-ship, Jeret is a libation artist who is responsible for the creation of one of The Esquire's most popular drinks, the Mas Chingoni, a spin-off of the traditional Negroni cocktail with a few key ingredient changes.

We recommend you grab a Mas Chingoni, head out onto the back deck and enjoy the view. Even better, make reservations well ahead of time and enjoy a table on the deck during the yearly "Taste of the River Walk."

http://youtu.be/m8jB7rRUriA

NEARBY DISTRACTIONS

The San Antonio River Walk

www.thesanantonioriverwalk.com

(always open, though restaurant, bar and shop hours vary by location).

Probably the most famous of San Antonio's tourist attractions, the River Walk is a network of pedestrian walkways one story beneath the streets of downtown San Antonio. The paths follow the San Antonio River and are lined with just about every kind of bar/restaurant (including The Esquire) in the city ensuring something for everyone.

Ranger Creek Brewing & Distilling

www.drinkrangercreek.com

4834 Whirlwind Dr. San Antonio, TX 78217 (210) 775-2099
(tour times and dates vary; call or check their website).

Claiming the title of the only "brewstillery" in Texas, Ranger Creek both brews beer and makes Texas Bourbon Whiskey. Featuring once-a-month tours, for those interested in getting a look at how they make beer and whiskey, plus daily samplings, it is worth the short 13-mile drive from the Esquire.

Little Red Barn

www.littleredbarnsteakhouse.com

1902 South Hackberry San Antonio, TX 78210 (210) 532-4235
(Monday-Thursday 11am-2pm & 4:30pm-9pm, Friday 11am-2pm & 4:30pm-10pm, Saturday 12am-10pm, Sunday 11:30am-8pm).

In the mood for steak? Then head over to the Little Red Barn Steakhouse, which is only three miles from The Esquire. Established in 1963 and claiming to be the largest steakhouse in Texas the Little Red Barn has great steaks, fast service, picnic-style seating and an authentic Texas atmosphere, making for a unique and fun dining experience.

THE MENGER BAR

SAN ANTONIO, TX

204 Alamo Plaza
San Antonio, TX 78205
1-800-345-9285
http://mengerhotel.com/
http://youtu.be/GroSRcM8eoc

Food: Yes
Live Music: No
Hours: Monday—Friday 11am-12am,
Saturday—Sunday 12pm-12am
Type of Bar: Pub
What to Drink: The house margarita or a Lone Star
Why You Should Go: More cattle deals struck here than
anywhere else in the United States, plus the legacy of
Teddy Roosevelt, and the Alamo is literally right next door.

The Menger Bar and Hotel, located just feet from San Antonio's world-famous River Walk and next to the Alamo, has been around for more than 150 years and has a history that would make some *countries* jealous....

HISTORY

Built on the site of Texas's first brewery (the Menger Brewery) and across the street from the Alamo, the Menger Hotel was originally opened in 1859—just 13 years after Texas was admitted to the Union and a short 23 years after the battle of the Alamo. It was originally built as a 50-room hotel and dubbed "the finest hotel west of the Mississippi," but its popularity grew at such a dramatic rate that a three-story addition had to be built just after opening. Just like any high-end establishment of the time it also contained a spectacular and extravagant bar.

The bar itself was built in 1887 and is an exact replica of London's now-demolished House of Lord's Pub. Dark cherry wood, beveled mirrors from France, decorated glass cabinets, and brass spittoons created a bar of rare sophistication. That isn't to say it didn't attract a wide range of clientele. From Presidents, to generals, cattle barons, writers and poets, this bar has seen them all...and more.

Teddy Roosevelt recruited some of the famous Rough Riders (the US volunteer cavalry of the Spanish-American War) right here in the Menger Hotel. During a particular set of drills Roosevelt was so impressed with these men he ordered an early end to the day and declared drinks on him at their favorite bar, which just so happened to be the Menger. Teddy was later reprimanded for his actions by his Colonel, who stated that an officer drinking with his men was not conducive to good discipline.

Teddy accepted the reprimand and left the tent. Within minutes he returned to the Colonel's tent, saluted, and then declared "Sir, I consider myself the damnedest ass within ten miles of this camp! Good night, sir!"

Along the walls of the bar and the hotel you'll find a huge assortment of photos showing some of the more prominent guests to have visited the Menger. Included are Presidents Theodore Roosevelt, Ulysses S. Grant, Woodrow Wilson, and Dwight D. Eisenhower.

Other guests have included Robert E. Lee, George Patton, Oscar Wilde, Jimmy Doolittle and even baseball great Babe Ruth (put simply, the list is distinguished). One could spend hours viewing the photos and memorabilia throughout the hotel.

TODAY

The Menger Bar is a favorite stop-off for tourists, who wander in from the heat after perusing the nearby Alamo. At times the small bar can feel a bit crowded as a tour bus drops people off right outside the door, but they generally fade away to view the rest of the hotel. The bar is also a favorite of local or visiting celebrities, so be on the lookout.

An unusual feature is the upstairs, loft-like seating area. We'd prefer to sit at the bar, but you should walk up and take in the different perspective it affords of the entire room. It's also nice to think about all of the deals that were struck here between ranchers long ago.

In addition to prominent guests from its past, some guests and employees decided to never leave. The Menger, like so many of the establishments we've visited, is rumored to have its fair share of ghosts. We were told it has a ghost from every era, including the ghost of Richard King, The King Ranch founder and time-to-time Menger guest, Sallie White, a previous house keeper, and even a Confederate soldier. Experiences range from smelling cigar smoke in rooms, the feeling of being tucked into bed, hearing the expression "pardon me" when no one is near you, and the occasional call for room service from empty rooms.

THE FOOD

The Hotel has an upscale restaurant—the Colonial Room Restaurant—that you can order from while sitting in the bar.

It features many of the entrees you'd expect to find in a San Antonio eatery—steak, fish, chicken and some pastas.

THE DRINKS

When you walk into the Menger Bar you would expect the drink menu to reflect the sophistication. But in this case looks can be deceiving. If you have a more refined palate and are looking for a martini or Old Fashioned you will be well served here, but if you are a fan of the everyday bottle of cold beer or a nice margarita, then you've definitely come to the right place.

There are really two drinks you need to try here. The first is a bottle of Lone Star and the second is their house margarita.

Lone Star is a Texas favorite, founded and brewed in the expansive state, is served ice cold and is perfect on a hot and

humid summer day in San Antonio. The house margarita is made in the traditional manner, with fresh ingredients, and is one of the best, if not the best in all the state.

NEARBY DISTRACTIONS

The Alamo
www.thealamo.org
300 Alamo Plaza San Antonio, Texas 78205 (866) 769-8419 (Monday-Saturday 9am-5:30pm, Sunday
10am-5:30pm, except Christmas).

Directly across the street from the Menger sits the world-renowned Alamo. Home of the Battle of the Alamo, where all but two defenders were killed, it was on these hallowed grounds that while ultimately defeated, Texans found a common rallying point and beat Santa Anna's army.

Ripley's Believe It Or Not
www.ripleys.com/sanantonio
301 Alamo Plaza San Antonio, TX 78205 (210) 224-9299 (Sunday-Thursday 10am-7pm,
Friday-Saturday 10am-10pm).

Sitting across the street from the Menger as well as from the Alamo is San Antonio's Ripley's Believe It Or Not. Featuring artifacts, stories and images that will blow you away, it is sure to be fun for anyone.

Chunky's Burgers

4602 Callaghan Rd. San Antonio, TX 78228 (210) 433-9960 (Tuesday-Thursday 11am-9pm, Friday 11am-10pm, Saturday 11:30am-10pm, Sunday 12pm-6pm)

Up for a challenge? Then head over to Chunky's Burgers & More, about 11 miles away, to tackle the Four Horsemen Challenge! To win all you have to do is consume a half a pound of beef with the Ghost Chile in under 25 minutes. Good luck!

OTHER NOTABLE AREA BARS

VFW Post 76
**10 10th St San Antonio, TX 78215 (210) 223-4581
(Monday-Thursday 9am-10pm, Friday-Saturday 9am-12am).**

That's right: we're suggesting a VFW post. Why? Because it's the oldest post in Texas, of course. But more than that, this place actually has some great history attached to the Menger Bar and San Antonio in general. The post was founded in 1904 by veterans of the Spanish-American war. The hundred-year-old house was donated to them in 1946 and is a museum of the military history of the area. If you want a history lesson while knocking back Lone Star beers, this is a great place to get it.

Buckhorn Saloon
**318 East Houston Street San Antonio, TX 78205
(210) 247-4000 (Monday-Sunday 11am-varied, call
for closing times).**

The saloon was founded in 1881 and is a good slice of San Antonio's history. Be advised that the "museum" portion really is little more than a tourist trap, with $20 prices to see some stuffed animals (you can see a better collection at the Buckhorn Exchange in Denver for the price of a drink). The saloon, though, is the real deal, and there's no charge for admittance. It's rumored that Pancho Villa planned his revolution here, and that Teddy Roosevelt stopped in for a drink.

EL PASO AREA

There are few Wild West towns in the United States that are as overlooked as El Paso, Texas. While places like Tombstone and Dodge City garner the imagination of Hollywood screenwriters, El Paso, with its much more interesting and amazing history, seems to go completely unnoticed.

But in fact, this area was awash in the factual accounts of what we normally think of as movie fiction.

Brothels abounded in the city, and there are dozens of true tales of madams who killed their lovers, themselves or someone else. Shoot-outs on the street were a regular occurrence, with many putting legendary shootouts you've heard of (like the gunfight at the OK Corral) to pitiful shame.

The most deadly gun in the West, outlaw gunfighter John Wesley Hardin, walked El Paso's streets and—ironically enough—practiced law. He also met his end here in the form of a bullet through his head from another gunfighter.

Throughout the region are found stories like this, all of them true, and most of them you've probably never heard of.

Another point to consider about the region is that just on

the other side of the river from El Paso is a city that's rivaling the most dangerous cities in the world. Juarez, Mexico, has been locked in a bloody drug war for the past five years. In 2010 they reached a high of 3,111 murders, which fell to a still-staggering 1,955 in 2011. And these are only the ones people have reported or seen.

The area covered here is large, and it will take some driving to get to all of the bars on the list. But they are well worth it.

TRANSPORTATION: The public transportation of the region is fairly limited. The area is also fairly spread out, so renting a car is a must, especially when travelling from El Paso north up the Rio Grande valley. Three places are within walking distance of each other, but a designated driver is a good idea, especially considering you'll be driving on narrow farm roads. In El Paso Yellow Cab (915) 533-3433 (Monday-Sunday 24hrs). United Independent Cab Company (915) 590-8294 (Monday-Sunday 24hrs). In Mesilla Las Cruces Shuttle and Taxi (575) 525-1784 (Monday-Sunday 9am-10pm).

ROSA'S CANTINA

EL PASO, TX

3454 Doniphan Drive
El Paso, TX 79922
(915) 833-0402
http://youtu.be/ms9I4OWY6zU

Food: Yes
Live Music: Yes
Hours: Monday—Sunday 11am-1am
Type of Bar: Saloon
What to Drink: A bottle of Lone Star and a shot of Cuervo
Why You Should Go: The song by Marty Robbins, El Paso, was written based on this place. What more do you need?

Rosa's Cantina is perhaps what most people think of when they think Wild West saloon. It haunts the songs and sounds of generations of singers and writers ever since it was first mentioned by Robbins. For some, coming here is a pilgrimage, but no bucket list of bars would be complete without seeing this place.

THE HISTORY

Rosa's wasn't always Rosa's. It was actually founded in the early 1940s (by the name of Los Tigres) outside of El Paso in what was called Smelter-town (so named because of the many factories and smelters in the area). It was a quiet neighborhood bar like any other until 1957 when it was bought by Beto and Anita Zubia. That started a chain of events that would put the place on the map for years to come.

One of the first things Zubia did was change the name, liking the sound of "Rosa's Cantina" after one of his waitresses, and the name stuck. Then, a by-chance stop when the place was closed one day created a legend and the reason why people flock to it today.

The story goes that Marty Robbins was driving from Nashville to Phoenix when he and his crew happened upon Rosa's Cantina. At the time the main road taking travelers from west Texas to southern New Mexico passed right in front of the bar. According to legend Marty stopped, got out of the car and looked around and then, inspired, got back in the car and headed to Phoenix.

By the time he hit Phoenix the song, "El Paso", was complete.

The song tells the story of a cowboy who falls in love with a Mexican dancing girl. In a jealous rage he shoots a potential suitor and then flees the bar to the badlands of New Mexico. Drawn back by his love he crosses back into Texas on his way to Rosa's but is chased and shot by a posse. His love, Felina, witnesses the cowboy's valiant effort to make it back to her and runs to comfort him as he lies dying.

One thing you must do if you find yourself heading to Rosa's is actually listen to the song. Marty talks about the badlands of New Mexico, easily viewable right across the street from Rosa's. He also talks about looking down on the town of El Paso from the badlands, easily imaginable looking at the hills in the distance.

TODAY

Historically Rosa's wasn't always the most inviting place for out-siders. Take for example the time Beto Zubia locked all of the doors because a couple of buses loaded with college athletes and tourists pulled up expecting to visit the world-renowned estab-lishment. He and the regulars sat quietly as the out-of-towners knocked on the doors. When asked why he did it, Zubia said it was because they would have drunk all the beer.

Today Rosa's is a more welcoming saloon, with a mix of locals, celebrities, and tourist from all over the world. Some of the more recognizable names to frequent Rosa's are Chip Woolley (trainer of 50-to-1 long shot Kentucky Derby-winner

Mine That Bird), Don Haskins (who coached the first integrated college basketball team to a national title), and of course Marty Robbins. Rosa's spends most of its daylight hours as a restaurant, getting especially busy during the Sunland Park winter racing season. The evenings find Rosa's transformed into a traditional bar, hosting live bands from all over the country and a busy dance floor.

When you go do keep in mind that despite its legacy this is still a locals' bar. One regular we talked to had been going there for lunch for 35 years. We asked him how often he hears the song by Robbins, and he shot us a look Clint Eastwood typically reserves for guys he's about to put an end to. If the place is empty, play the song. If it's crowded, abstain and wait for some other sucker to put the money in and draw the menacing stares from the locals.

THE FOOD

Rosa's kitchen is run by 30-year veteran Martha, who says the secret to making good Mexican food is love. If that is true, she must pour her entire heart into every meal she prepares: the food is great.

The most popular and most recommended plate is the Mexican Plate. The plate, both colorful and generous, gives you a wide range of excellent Mexican food, from tacos to enchiladas, along with beans, rice, and chips and salsa. It is a must-try when you stop in.

THE DRINKS

Until recently Rosa's had a limited liquor license, which only allowed them to serve beer and wine. However, they now have a full liquor license and feature a full bar with most easy-to-make cocktails at the ready.

For a recommended drink we suggest either a Lone Star beer and/or a shot of Cuervo. These are the cheapest beer and shots you can get just about anywhere, and for that that reason alone, the idea is appealing.

NEARBY DISTRACTIONS

Sunland Park Racetrack & Casino
www.sunland-park.com
1200 Futurity Dr. Sunland Park, NM 88063, (575) 874-5200 (operating hours vary by season, live racing occurs December-April).

Though it's less than two miles from Rosa's Cantina, Sunland Park Racetrack and Casino is in a whole other city and state. Featuring live horse racing December to April and a casino open throughout the year, a stop here will help to give you the total Rosa's Cantina experience. 50-1 odds Kentucky Derby-winner Mine That Bird's trainer used to frequent Rosa's and the racetrack is located in what is considered the "Badlands" of New Mexico as described in Marty Robbins' song, "El Paso".

The State Line
www.countyline.com/StateLine.html
1222 Sunland Park Dr. Sunland Park, El Paso TX (915) 581-3371 (Monday-Thursday 11:30am-9:30pm, Friday-Saturday 11:30am-10:00pm, Sunday 11:30am-9pm).

Where else can you park in Texas, eat in New Mexico and pee in either? Less than two miles from Rosa's, and right next door to Sunland Park Racetrack, is the State Line Restaurant. Featuring tasty BBQ, Texas-sized helpings, and outstanding beef ribs while straddling New Mexico and Texas, it's a great place to stop if you are craving BBQ.

The Plaza Theatre

www.theplazatheatre.org

125 Pioneer Plaza El Paso, TX 79901 (915) 231-1100 (operating hours vary by show, call or visit their website).

Though it's a lengthy 25-mile drive from Rosa's to the Plaza Theatre, if you're in the area long enough it's worth the drive. Opened in 1930, no expense was spared in the creation of this legendary and lavish theatre: the largest theatre between Dallas and Los Angeles upon completion. Recently renovated, today it continues to be a must-see destination, hosting popular performances from all over the globe. Tours are offered weekly, so plan ahead if you'd like to attend.

CHOPE'S BAR

LA MESA, NM

16145 New Mexico 28
La Mesa, NM 88044
(575) 233-3420
http://youtu.be/Amr6Q37MQ-c

Food: Yes
Live Music: No
Hours: Monday—Sunday 2pm-10pm
Type of Bar: Dive
What to Drink: 40 ounce beer
Why You Should Go: Great history, excellent New
Mexico food, wonderful people and atmosphere.

Chope's is a legendary bar and restaurant located just north of El Paso, Texas in the tiny New Mexico town of La Mesa. The small bar is the essence of a roadhouse dive, and is one of the must-see places in the Southwest. Sitting next to a mayor or migrant farm-worker and swapping stories with foul-smelling bikers is all in an afternoon's jaunt to Chope's!

THE HISTORY

Chope's, named after Chope Benavides, the long-time owner of the bar and restaurant, was founded in 1915 by Chope's mother, Longina Benavides. She originally began cooking and selling food to local farmers and their hired help. Because of her arthritis she couldn't cook on a regular basis, so when she felt able and had meals prepared she would hang a lantern outside of her house to let surrounding neighbors know her kitchen was open.

There was no bar in those days, but during Prohibition the ever-enterprising Longina saw a need not being met and so made moonshine to sell to those same farmers and their employees.

Once Prohibition ended, the restaurant became official and soon thereafter the bar was opened in the same small house.

In the early 1940s Chope took over the business, which at that time had grown into a small but thriving "local's" joint. One of his first moves was to build a small building about 30 feet north of the house to contain the growing bar. This was done to keep his daughters (living in the house) from overhearing the language used in the bar by the local laborers.

TODAY

Chope's is probably one of the most beloved bars and restaurants we've been to. Locals will tell you about their first drink there, about the time their parents met there, and so on and so forth. What's more, the crowd is about as diverse as they come. On any given afternoon you'll find college students, farmers, bikers, politicians, New Mexicans, Texans and families from all walks of life enjoying the great food in the restaurant or 40's and pitchers of Margaritas in the bar. No one is out of place here as long as they behave themselves and are respectful of each other.

THE FOOD

It's tough to talk about the food at Chope's and really do it any sort of justice. The place makes arguably the best New Mexican

food in all of Southern New Mexico, West Texas, Arizona, California and quite possibly the United States. What they do best are their chile rellenos—roasted green chiles stuffed with white cheese and then battered and deep-fried. People flock from all over the world to try these and they've been acclaimed by just about every online and offline journal or blog about food that there is. Give these a try smothered in the green chile (with a glass of milk standing by).

THE DRINKS

Chope's is the only bar we have ever been to (which is saying a lot) that sells 40-ounce bottles of beer. Chope started serving the 40's to attract college students from the local colleges and (surprise, surprise) it worked. College students quickly became a fixture in both the restaurant and the bar and to this day it is a rite of passage to make the short but scenic drive from El Paso to Chope's in La Mesa, New Mexico, to drink a 40 oz. either close to your 21st birthday or shortly after arriving in the area. When you order one, tell the bartender, "no glass," and then drink from the bottle.

NEARBY DISTRACTIONS

Drive Through Stahmann Farms
Located between Mesilla and Chope's on Hwy 28 (the Don Juan de Oñate Trail), is the picturesque Stahmann Farm pecan orchards.

At over 3200 acres, the farm is one of the largest in the world. Huge pecan trees form a beautiful arbor over the road stretching for miles leading to a beautiful drive. Though beautiful anytime of the year, the summer is the most spectacular when the trees are green and the shade provided brings a welcome respite from the often intense heat. A must-see if you are ever in the area.

Rio Grande Vineyards & Winery
www.riograndwinery.com
5321 Highway 28 at Mile Marker 25 Las Cruces, NM 88005
(575) 524-3985 (wine tasting Friday-Sunday 12pm-5:30pm or by appointment).

A pleasant nine mile drive through Stahmann pecan farm and just north of Chope's is the Rio Grande Vineyards & Winery. Featuring 10 different European grape varieties, they offer a full

complement of white and red wines. Tastings are fun and informative with plenty of time spent helping tasters discover wines
geared toward their unique pallet.

PALACIO BAR

MESILLA, NM

2600 Avenida De Mesilla
Mesilla, NM 88046
(575) 525-2910
http://youtu.be/Z3hglXrPlXo

Food: No
Live Music: Yes
Hours: Monday—Wednesday, Sunday 12pm-11pm,
Thursday 12pm-12am, Friday—Saturday 12pm-12:30am
Type of Bar: Saloon
What to Drink: Tequila shots a lá Velia Chavez
Why You Should Go: To experience not only the history
of small, border town life, but also a place that is only 20
years removed from a truly male-dominated world.

40 miles north of El Paso off Highway 28 in the small village of Mesilla, New Mexico, Palacio Bar draws a mainly Mexican-American crowd to listen to music, dance and share a culture pretty unfamiliar to the rest of the world. This is a great place with the genuine flavor only a true neighborhood bar can contain.

THE HISTORY

When it comes to great beginnings, Palacio Bar has to be one of the most interesting we have heard of. In 1936, the building that currently houses Palacio's was being constructed by Pablo Salcido and his father as a new building for their blacksmith shop. On one particular Saturday, Pablo's wife decided to have a dance and invite all of the locals from the nearby village of Mesilla, New Mexico. The initial dance was a huge success and, at the request of the locals, they continued to host dances the following weeks and months. As the dances continued to gain popularity, Pablo's wife became inspired.

She convinced Pablo to convert the blacksmith shop into a bar and dance hall and they set about turning it into the area's most popular night and weekend spot. A bar was installed, the concrete floors were covered with wood, and Salcido's dance hall was officially opened. A short time later Pablo renamed the business Palacio Bar and Café.

In 75 years Palacio's has seen a lot. One of the more unusual periods in its span didn't end until founder Pablo passed away in 1991. Up until that point, women weren't allowed in the bar.

Think about that for a moment. In the 1970s McSorley's Old Ale House in New York City was sued by a women's rights group and the case went all the way to the Supreme Court so they could gain entrance to the male-only holdout of the Bowery.

But women weren't allowed into Palacio's for 20 years after the case was settled. When we asked his daughter why he didn't want women in the bar she said she believed her father just didn't want to make mixed drinks.

The bar was almost closed when in August of 1991 a fire severely damaged the entire building. Luckily it's made out of adobe—mud bricks—and so only the interior was damaged while the exterior remained standing. However, the State of New Mexico gave them only a month to clean, rebuild and get back into business before they'd yank the liquor license. As a testament to the importance of a place like this in the community,

the locals volunteered time and talent to rebuild the bar and get them back to serving in less than a month.

TODAY

Today Palacio's is still an important landmark of the Mesilla community. During the day it's a quiet local's bar where retired and working community members meet to discuss everything from politics to this year's green chile crop (which grow a stone's throw away). At night, it transforms into what it started out as: a dance hall. Velia Chavez, Pablo Salcido's daughter and now owner, spends a lot of her time scouting for bands to perform there and does her best to mix it up with everything from country to salsa to rock.

While Veila isn't as strict as her father (she does let women in), she does have some rules to follow. Don't expect to show up and be let in while wearing "colors;" if you're caught dancing in a manner she deems inappropriate then out you go; and if you are considered to be dressed inappropriately (short skirt, revealing shirt, etc) don't expect to even get in the door.

THE DRINKS

If you happen to make it to Palacio's, the absolute must-try drink is the Tarantula Tequila. It's a favorite of owner Velia, who showed us how to drink it "correctly."

Tarantula isn't a typical tequila: it's blended with fruits and liqueur, giving it a citrus taste mixed with the familiar mescal

of the tequila. Forget the lime and the salt and, if it isn't already served with one, ask for an orange slice.

While it is not an expensive bottle of tequila, it is very good and has become one of the few tequilas we would recommend shooting.

http://youtu.be/lSuJC4rLu8g

NEARBY DISTRACTIONS

Mesilla Valley Bosque State Park
www.emnrd.state.nm.us
5000 Calle del Norte, Mesilla, NM 88046 (575) 523-4398
(Monday-Sunday 8am-5pm with some seasonal variations)

Located a short 3.5-mile drive from Palacio's is the Mesilla Valley Bosque State Park. Featuring a short 1.4 mile hiking trail, wildlife viewing, visitor center, amphitheater and educational programs, the park gives visitors an opportunity to learn about local plants and animals along the famous Rio Grande River.

Luna Rossa Winery

www.lunarossawinery.com

1321 Avenida de Mesilla Las Cruces, NM 88005 (575) 526-2484 (Monday—Thursday 10am-9pm, Friday—Saturday 10am-10pm, Sunday 10am-8pm).

Less than a mile from Palacio's is one of Luna Rosa Winery's tasting rooms. Luna Rossa was founded in 2001 by Paola and Sylvia D'Andrea. Paola is from the Friuli region in northeast Italy and is passionate both about proving the desert can produce grapes successfully and about creating an outstanding selection of New Mexico wines.

St. Clair Winery & Bistro

www.stclairwinery.com

1720 Avenida de Mesilla Las Cruces, NM 88005 (575) 524-2408 (Sunday—Thursday 11am-9pm, Friday—Saturday 11am-10pm).

Also less than a mile from Palacio's is St. Clair's Winery and Bistro. A landmark since 1984, their vineyard is located in the Mimbres Valley in Deming, New Mexico, to take advantage of the area's warm days and cool nights. They produce some of the best grapes in New Mexico including cabernet sauvignon, chardonnay, sauvignon blanc, zinfandel and others. Their outstanding wine in combination with their excellent menu and a relaxing patio make for a great way to spend the evening.

CORN EXCHANGE AT LA POSTA DE MESILLA

MESILLA, NM

2410 Calle De San Albino
Mesilla, NM 88046
(575) 524-3524
http://www.laposta-de-mesilla.com
http://youtu.be/h2jUd60Tmuo

Food: Yes
Live Music: No
Hours: Tuesday—Thursday, Sunday 11am-9pm,
Friday—Saturday 11am-9:30pm
Type of Bar: Saloon
What to Drink: Fine tequila on rocks or a Chilerita
Why You Should Go: The sheer history of the place,
stand in the footsteps of western legends, like Billy the
Kid, Ulysses S. Grant and others.

Júst around the corner from two other Bucket List Bars™, and about 40 miles north of El Paso, Texas, is a cantina that really reflects the spirit of the Old West. The cantina, which existed in at least the mid-19th century but was re-established in 1939 (and more recently remodeled), is unique simply because of the history and ambiance.

THE HISTORY

La Posta dates back to the 1840s when it was a freight and passenger service station known as the Corn Exchange. It was located on the Pinos Altos stagecoach line and was owned and operated by the Bean brothers. In the 1850s it became a critical stop for the Butterfield Overland Stagecoach and featured the Corn Exchange hotel, one of the finest hotels in the Southwest during the 1870s and 1880s.

The hotel hosted such guests as President Ulysses S. Grant, who according to the original guest book, never paid for his room, frontiersman and Indian fighter, Kit Carson, Mexican revolutionary Pancho Villa, and—while it cannot be confirmed—it is rumored that the notorious outlaw Billy the Kid was a guest at the hotel as well. In addition to the hotel, the complex hosted a fine dining restaurant, the cantina—at that time called the Bean Saloon (so named for the original owners)—a blacksmith shop, a mercantile, a stable and even a local school house.

In 1939 local entrepreneur and niece of the owner, Katy Griggs Camunez, purchased the saloon and restaurant portion from her cousin for "one dollar and love and affection." She set up a small dining room on the dirt floor and began cooking and selling regional Mexican food. The small enterprise grew into the large restaurant and cantina found today.

TODAY

Today La Posta is the only building left from the original Butterfield Overland Stagecoach route, and through years of growth and acquisitions it has expanded to occupy the entire original Corn Exchange complex of over 10,000 square feet. Upon entering the complex you will find yourself greeted by exquisite southwestern décor, tropical birds and, due to a new legislative measure, some of the last remaining piranhas in New Mexico.

We recommend you take some time to walk around the restaurant and bar to get a feel for the place, being careful to not get lost in the expansive and confusing halls and rooms. A couple of things to look for are the old (and for the most part, original) ceilings and adobe brick walls, the original blacksmith shop with fireplace still installed, the Bean Saloon and the original La Posta restaurant that is located just off of the bar.

Once you've explored the building, retire to the Corn Exchange Cantina for drinks and atmosphere. Remember that in this small room you'd be drinking with some of the most legendary characters from the old west.

The crowd at La Posta is as diverse as its history. You'll find college students, professors, farmers, tourists, locals, politicians, artists, musicians and everything in between. As a matter of fact, during our visit New Mexico Governor Susana Martinez arrived to have a working lunch with some of the local business owners and community leaders (sadly, we weren't invited).

THE FOOD

La Posta features a mainly Southern New Mexican menu with food made from scratch, served hot, quickly and includes generous portions.

We highly recommend the spicy shrimp cocktail—more of a Bloody Mary than a traditional shrimp cocktail, especially when ordered with a side-shot of tequila (added to the cocktail, not drunk).

Another highly popular menu item is the tostada compustas, three corn tortillas fried and shaped into small cups and then filled with an assortment of chile, including their famous red chile meat (which they make in a very traditional manner from local chile pods).

Finally, we also suggest the fajitas brought sizzling to your table with all of the garnishes and trimmings.

THE DRINKS

The featured drink at the Corn Exchange Cantina is the Chilerita, a twist on the traditional Margarita. It's made with fresh squeezed lime juice, Patron's orange liqueur, Hornitos tequila, house sweet and sour mix, and a blackberry habanero sauce called Besito Caliente.

It's the habenero sauce that makes this drink so different and tasty. The drink is sweet to be sure, but tempered of course with the tequila. The unique part comes at the end of a drink, when the heat from the sauce kind of slowly drizzles down your throat. It is a great twist on a traditional drink.

Now granted Ulysses S. Grant and Billy the Kid wouldn't have had Margaritas. However, considering the proximity to the border, they would have been drinking what used to be known as mescal wine or mescal brandy—now known as tequila. The cantina features over 100 tequilas, enough to find something for even the most distinguished tequila connoisseur. Try one in a glass neat or on the rocks and sip it while taking in the history.

http://youtu.be/BE2W9SMMj98

NEARBY DISTRACTIONS

Mesilla Plaza

www.oldmesilla.org/html/the_plaza.html

Located in the heart of Mesilla and mere feet from the door to La Posta is Mesilla Plaza, which was originally created by the concentration of the town's population for defense against Apache raiders.

You will find the San Albino Basilica, founded in 1851, and a monument celebrating the consummation of the Gadsden Purchase that took place here in this very plaza in 1853. You'll also find that many of the same buildings and structures that were built here in the 1800s still exist, but feature gift shops, galleries and restaurants. No trip to Mesilla is complete without · visiting the Plaza.

Trinity Site
www.wsmr.army.mil/PAO/Trinity
Visit website for directions to site (575) 678-1134
(open twice a year to visitors).

The Trinity Site is where the first atomic bomb was tested during the early morning hours of July 16th, 1945. The event and the discovery of the atomic explosion led to a quick end of World War 2, a new age in electric production and a terrifying dynamic with Russia during the Cold War. Though it's a lengthy three-hour drive from La Posta and only open to the public two times per year, a visit here is a glimpse into America's scientific ingenuity and a world-altering discovery. Definitely worth the time if you're here when it's open.

 # EL PATIO

MESILLA, NM

2171 Calle De Parian
Mesilla, NM 88046
(575) 526-9943
http://youtu.be/vUSXiqApHYA

Food: No
Live Music: Yes
Type of Bar: Dive
Hours: Monday—Tuesday 4pm-2am, Wednesday—Saturday 2pm-2am, Sunday 12pm-12am
What Type to Drink: Cheapest beer they have, preferably PBR
Why You Should Go: Housed in a building from 1870 that's seen Billy the Kid through it, great Southwestern history, and is the quintessential dive bar.

The story of this dive bar, about 40 miles north of El Paso in the small village of Mesilla, is the story of the man whose family still runs it. He was the attorney that represented Billy the Kid when he was charged with the murder of a Mesilla Valley Sheriff, a newspaper editor and publisher, and the unfortunate subject of a murder mystery.

THE HISTORY

Albert J. Fountain was a Colonel in the Union Army during the Civil War. Originally from San Francisco, he moved to Mesilla, New Mexico, after the war to run a newspaper and law office. He opened shop in an adobe building on the corner of Calle de Parian and Calle Princessa. In January of 1896, Fountain and his youngest son Henry traveled to Lincoln County, New Mexico to assist in the prosecution of a suspected cattle rustler. On Feb. 1st, 1896, they loaded their horse drawn carriage for the day's trip back to Mesilla. They were never seen or heard from again and the only things found were the horses, the carriage, shell casings and two pools of blood. They had just vanished.

Fast forward to 1934 and the Fountain family had maintained ownership of the building now housing El Patio. At that time a young Art Fountain was an up and coming engineering student at nearby New Mexico A&M (New Mexico State University today). While discussing his plans for the future with one of his professors, he was discouraged from pursuing a career in engineering due to his Hispanic heritage. Art took this rather racist advice and on the heels of Prohibition opened El Patio Bar in 1934.

From 1934 until today the bar has been owned and operated by the Fountain family while being passed on from father to son. The bar has always been a hot spot for local, national and international bands, and during the last 77 years it's hosted more than its fair share of celebrities, surprising given the bar's location in a small and out-of-the-way town. According to the current owner, celebrities like James Earl Jones, the Blues Brothers, and even Clint Eastwood have stopped by.

TODAY

Today El Patio can be described in two words: Dive Bar. The dark interior is a hodgepodge of mismatched tables, chairs, southwestern murals, mounted deer heads and even the quintessential Christmas-tree lights. The building itself, well over 125 years old, is authentic southwestern architecture and just seeing the exposed mud bricks is worth the stop.

There's a small stage that still features an assembly of bands that run the gamut from punk to ska and country.

The crowd is similarly varied, with university professors, artists, students and professionals mixing it up together. The staff is no-nonsense and typically harried by the large crowds that can pour in on weekend nights.

Day or night though it is a great place to step into, breathe in that dive bar smell, enjoy a cold beer, check out the dozens of photos of all the great talent that has come through and catch some great bands. If you happen to run into Al Fountain, offer to buy him a beer and invite him to sit down; he has some great stories to tell about the history of the bar, the history of the town and most interestingly the history of Billy the Kid (who in his time would have walked through this building).

THE DRINKS

As with a lot of other dive bars, El Patio isn't really known for their specialty in a particular alcohol or mixed drink. They do have a full bar and some talented bartenders, but then again the place also serves a big college crowd. In other words think simple, like a beer and a shot over martinis or more sophisticated drinks.

Their beer selection also isn't that extensive, but it is cheap.

Go with whatever is on special, or if nothing is on special then just go with the cheapest beer they have. It will be a fitting

tribute to both the great history of the building and to the dive bar of dive bars that now resides there.

NEARBY DISTRACTIONS

White Sands National Monument
www.nps.gov/whsa
19955 U.S. 70 Alamogordo, NM 88310,
(575) 479-6124 (operating hours vary and unexpected closures due to missile testing are to be expected, call or visit website)

About an hour's drive east of Mesilla is the White Sands National Monument. Featuring over 275 square miles of white sand dunes, it's the world's largest gypsum dune field. It is also the last place that Colonel Albert J. Fountain (a onetime Billy the Kid lawyer and relative of El Patio's founder) and his eight-year-old son disappeared and are assumed murdered though the bodies were never recovered. White Sands is a fun and interesting place to visit, and if you can time your visit on a full moon night it's a once-in-a-lifetime experience watching the moon rise over the mountains and reflect off the white sand.

Gadsden Museum
1875 Boutz Rd. Mesilla, NM 88046 (575) 526-6293 (operating hours vary, call ahead for hours or an appointment).

Less than a five-minute walk from El Patio is the Gadsden Museum. Run by a descendant of Colonel Albert J. Fountain, it's described as "a charming trip back to the history of southern

New Mexico and the Mesilla Valley." Be sure to call ahead to find out the hours or set an appointment as there are no official hours and no website.

Fountain Theater
www.mesillavalleyfilm.org
2469 Calle De Guadelupe Mesilla, NM 88005 (575) 524-8287 (screening daily at 730 pm with matinees at 130 pm on Saturday and 230 pm on Sunday).

Located literally around the corner from El Patio is The Fountain Theatre. Built in 1905 on the site of a Confederate Army barracks, it is New Mexico's oldest continuously running movie house and originally featured both cinema and vaudeville performances. Today it includes alternative, foreign and independent films and features geared towards seasonal cult classics like Rosemary's Baby close to Halloween. Check the schedule before you arrive and you may be able to view one of your favorite classic movies on the big screen.

OTHER NOTABLE AREA BARS

Pershing Inn

2909 Pershing Drive El Paso, TX 79903 (915) 566-1331 (Monday-Sunday 12pm-2am).

Opened in 1949 this bar claims to have one of the first and oldest liquor licenses in El Paso, Texas. We have no idea how that's possible, considering the bar that turned into Rosa's Cantina had been there since the early 40s, but nevertheless. The place is a well-loved dive bar, filled with locals and not many tourists or visitors. Their drinks range from specialty margaritas to their take on classic cocktails. Be safe, go with beer.

Aceitunas Beer Garden

5200 Doniphan Drive El Paso, TX 79932 (915) 845-2277 (Tuesday-Thursday, Saturday 4pm-2am, Friday 3pm-2am).

It's kind of hard to think of an authentic beer garden in this dusty border city, but Aceitunas fits the bill perfectly. Featuring koi ponds, streams and tons of character, this El Paso staple has been serving the community for over 30 years. Their shtick is to be a beer garden, so expect loads of flowing beer, but they also feature a full bar (many of them in fact) so you'll be fine going for the Jagermeister instead of the PBR (assuming you are either a hipster or fraternity member).

DENVER

Denver, Colorado started as a stop on the route to supply nearby mining towns during the Pike's Peak gold rush of the 1850s and 1860s. As such it was a really wild place in its heyday. Like surrounding towns, Denver featured dozens of bars, alehouses and grocers where booze was had for cheap.

Granted, the booze may not have been that good, but it could be had at any rate. So, of course, could prostitutes and gambling.

During this time the town was becoming home to a number of immigrant groups, including the Irish, the Spanish and the Italian. What resulted was a melting pot not unlike many of the cities on the East Coast, with whole neighborhoods and sections of town that identified with one of these new populations.

There were also a number of famous characters that walked the streets of Denver in the 19th century. Men like Buffalo Bill Cody and Doc Holliday spent their time in the city's many gambling joints and brothels, as did the thousands of miners, travelers and cowboys bringing herds of cattle up from Texas.

While not as wild in the 20th century, Denver still saw its share of celebrities and sometimes dangerous episodes, with people like Jack Kerouac and Frank Sinatra making their way through (and stopping over at some of the bars we'll tell you about).

Denver grew into a major metropolis, now with over 600,000 people, major sports teams, music and concert arenas and, of course, some great places to drink.

TRANSPORTATION: Metro Taxi Denver (303) 333-3333 (Monday-Sunday 24hrs). Denver Airports Limousine (303) 719-3466 (Monday-Sunday 12pm-12:30am).

MY BROTHER'S BAR
DENVER, CO

2376 15th Street
Denver, CO 80202
(303) 455-9991
http://youtu.be/KgFoHR12kO4

Food: Yes
Live Music: No
Hours: Monday—Saturday 11am-2am
Type of Bar: Pub
What to Order: A craft beer or classic cocktail
Why You Should Go: This classic bar is a mainstay for Denver natives and is a throwback to another time—when bars were quiet places you went to talk to friends and strangers.

If you go to Denver you'll want to make it a point to come here. If you go on a Friday before 5:00 pm you can catch the notorious bartender Jimmy, who adds yet another layer of tradition and atmosphere to this already dripping-with-atmosphere Denver must-see.

THE HISTORY

My Brother's Bar, though known by another name at the time, was established in 1873 and is the oldest continuously operating bar in Denver, Colorado. Since that year booze has always been peddled out of this location. Both Jimmy the bartender and the owner, Jim Karagas, confirmed that the bar even operated through Prohibition (they both cited the lack of interest in enforcing Prohibition west of the Mississippi River).

The place has had its ups and downs. When first opened the neighborhood was mostly Italian Immigrants, and legend has it the very first Columbus Day celebration took place here, complete with parade. It lost a lot of its luster in the 1950s and 1960s though, becoming a dive bar and drawing a unique crowd, including Neal Cassady—Jack Kerouac's buddy and cohort.

Jim Karagas, the current owner, and his brother Orlando moved to Denver in 1968 and bought the bar shortly after their arrival, stating on more than one occasion that the bar was a dump when they first set eyes on it. In fact they bought it at night and never saw what it looked like during the day until it was too late.

The brothers spent the next few years cleaning up the bar

and returning it to its original appearance (minus an original upstairs floor, which had been removed long before they purchased the bar). A running joke about both the name of the place and the lack of a sign outside is that after they purchased it they couldn't think of what to call the place. When bill collectors, delivery men or patrons with questions would come in looking for the owner, James and his brother would tell them, "It's my brothers bar, go talk to him." This continued until the name finally stuck and the bar was referred to as My Brother's Bar permanently (although they still don't have a sign).

TODAY

The bar today will immediately remind you of a classic, Irish-style pub found on the East Coast, which is ironic considering the brothers were Greek. Nevertheless, you'll find gleaming mahogany and oak, classical music piped in through the stereo and a friendly atmosphere with a lot of locals and regulars.

There is also a patio out back if you'd like to soak in a nice Denver day, otherwise there's ample room to find a seat in either the bar area or a large room just next door.

The crowd is a mix of professionals from nearby office buildings, including state and city government employees, college students and Denver locals. We're told they're a regular spot for local sports celebrities, too, so bone up on your Rockies and Broncos players before arriving.

Something you may notice missing from the bar is the dull glow of any television. According to owner Jim and Jimmy the bartender, they have no televisions because they ruin the whole point of a bar. You can watch TV at home, but when you're at a bar you should be enjoying a good conversation with friends, family or even one of the many bartenders. After all, don't you go to a bar to enjoy the company of others?

THE FOOD

My Brothers Bar serves a lot of your typical bar food but with a few custom twists. The kitchen originally started with a very simple menu and only expanded slowly over the years and mainly through the use of their own employees' recipes. The most popular, and frequently imitated but never duplicated, is the JCB which stands for Jalapeno Cream Cheese Burger. It was created when Jim came in one morning to find Lana Harris, sister of NFL player Franco Harris, making some kind of cream cheese concoction. She was in the process of making Jalapeno Cream Cheese, which she then threw on a burger and gave it to Jim to try. It was on the menu the very next day.

Jimmy stated that on more than one occasion, they have had patrons come in, sit really close to the kitchen (it is connected to the end of the bar), order a JCB and watch with hawk-like intensity as it is prepared. They usually become quite flustered and even embarrassed when Jimmy asks them when *their* grand opening is and if they've figured out how to replicate the burger.

THE DRINKS

My Brothers Bar doesn't really have any signature drinks; rather the signature drink is actually the lack of certain drinks, or

more specifically, certain brands. When Jim first bought the bar, he tried to buy from both Coors and Budweiser. But as Mr. Karagas came to find out, his lack of large volume sales made Coors and Budweiser very unmotivated to make deliveries on time or sometimes at all.

After getting fed up with both brands, Jim decided to go with alternate brands, namely smaller and local breweries, and to this day will not serve or buy Budweiser or Coors products.

Today Budweiser and Coors both constantly bug Jim asking him to carry their beer but he sticks to his guns and refuses to carry any of their products. They still have some of the finest beers and spirits you could hope for; we recommend Golden City Red or Fuller's London Pride.

NEARBY DISTRACTIONS

REI

www.rei.com

1416 Platte St. Denver, CO 80202 (303) 756-3100 (Monday-Saturday 9am-9pm, Sunday 10am-7pm).

Located directly behind My Brother's Bar in the restored 1901 Denver Tramway building is one of REI's flagship stores. This place is huge, featuring a 47-foot monolith climbing wall offering a variety of climbing terrain, almost 95,000 square feet of outdoor adventurer shopping and a Starbucks. It's worth checking out just to see (or maybe try) the climbing wall and enjoy the view of the river from their deck.

Commons/Confluence Park

www.denvergov.org

2101 15th St. Denver, CO 80202

(720) 913-1311 (Hours vary by season).

Located directly across the river from My Brother's Bar is Common's Park. The park is nestled on the edge of downtown Denver and offers extensive paths and areas for picnics and sporting activities. But the true gem of the location is access to the Platte River. On a hot summer day there are few better activities than grabbing a tube to float down this small section of the river.

Denver Aquarium

www.aquariumrestaurants.com

700 Water Street Denver, CO 80211 (303) 561-4450 (Sunday-Thursday 10am-9pm,

Friday-Saturday 10am-9:30pm).

Taking the Colorado Front Range Trail, along the Platte River, the Denver Aquarium is a short half-mile walk from My Brother's Bar. Featuring extensive fresh and salt water aquariums, sharks, exotic and local fish and even a tiger exhibit, it leaves little to be desired (if you desire fish, that is). But for those who want to get a little closer to the life aquatic you can also dive with the sharks! In the middle of downtown Denver, certified or not, you can get up close and personal with sharks, barracudas, giant sea turtles and more. Just make sure you do this before visiting My Brother's Bar.

EL CHAPULTEPEC
DENVER, CO

1962 Market Street
Denver, CO 80202
(303) 295-9126
http://www.thepeclodo.com
http://youtu.be/dx9mGXtD_hk

Food: Yes
Live Music: Yes
Hours: Monday—Sunday 11am-1am
Type of Bar: Dive
What to Drink: Coors Banquet Beer
Why You Should Go: Best jazz bar west of the Mississippi, great history, wonderful Denver lore.

Opened on the 4th of July in 1933 and located at 20th and Market in Denver, Colorado, El Chapultepec, or The Pec as it is called locally, is among the best dive bars in the country. It's storied, has persona, attitude and is downright welcoming once you get past the initial fear and go inside.

THE HISTORY

The bar was founded by Tony Romano in what was at the time one of the grittier parts of Denver. Obtaining liquor license #2, The Pec originally opened as a mariachi joint serving Mexican food and catering to the local population of migrant workers. It obtained its tongue-twisting name after many of the workers asked Romano to cash their checks so they could send the money to their families, back in El Chapultepec, Mexico.

In 1958 the bar changed fairly dramatically when Romano's son-in-law, Jerry Krantz, took the place over. Jerry had developed a deep love of jazz music over the years and began featuring live jazz almost immediately. One of the first artists Jerry was able to book was Buddy Defranco, whose performance put The Pec on the map.

Over the next 40 years, the tiny, pink neon-lit bar played host to some of the biggest names in the history of jazz. Artists that played there included William (Count) Basie, the three Marsalis brothers, former president Bill Clinton and even Frank Sinatra himself. They and hundreds of local, national and international musicians played on the tiny stage making The Pec the unofficial capital of jazz west of the Mississippi.

Aside from the stories of Ella Fitzgerald listening to music in her limo parked in the alley, or of Jack Kerouac sitting quietly stoned in the booth immediately right of the front door, El Chapultepec really became famous because of Jerry Krantz himself. He was a hard-nosed bartender/owner/bouncer who took no shit from no one. He had a baseball bat behind the bar and was happy to tap some ne'er-do-well upside the head because, as he told us, "you gotta get their attention before you can talk to them."

Jerry passed in May, 2012, but his spirit doggedly lives on at this little-known treasure in Denver's former red light district.

TODAY

Jerry's daughter, Angela, has continued her father's legacy with only a few minor tweaks. She assured us that they no longer handle rowdy customers (or "assholes" as Jerry would refer to them) with a baseball bat. And while the bar still features the best live jazz bands they also mix in blues and funk (all live of course) for a change of pace. Other than that she's left things alone.

Visitors are greeted with a long, waist-high, Formica covered bar and glowing pink neon. Along the wall on the right are the booths so famous for hosting Kerouac and his band of miscreants in the early '50s. And at the end of the room is the famous stage, so tiny you wonder how the hell bands could fit up there. Be sure to take a look at all the famous headshots lining the wall. The tough guy standing next to the celebrities is Jerry.

The biggest change to The Pec is actually in the surrounding area. In 1995 the Colorado Rockies built Coors Field almost directly across the street from The Pec. The move was all part of the revitalization of Denver's downtown which included attracting new bars and restaurants to the surrounding areas. It's such a sharp contrast to see the building housing The Pec, squat and stucco, next to the taller, polished brick of the "revitalized" downtown.

THE FOOD

There is a small dining room with pool table just on the other side of the bar. The kitchen, featuring fairly traditional Mexican food—rice, beans, tacos and so forth—is located there and is a popular place to grab a bite while having a beer.

We didn't get to try them, but we hear the tamales are pretty outstanding. It's all relative, of course, when you combine the atmosphere, music and history of this place, everything tastes good.

THE DRINKS

The Pec holds Liquor License # 2, yet for some reason they never brag about it. In any case, think of this as your beer-and-shot bar, not the kind of place to make fancy shots or mixed drinks.

They also have the oldest Coors contract in Denver. In fact, the Coors family often let Jerry and his kids use their Sky Box at the next door stadium whenever they'd like. So aside from a shot of whiskey, get a Coors Banquet Beer for tradition's sake.

NEARBY DISTRACTIONS

Coors Field

colorado.rockies.mlb.com

2001 Blake Street Denver, CO 80205 (303) ROCKIES, (operating hours vary by game times and events).

Just steps from the front door of "The Pec" is Coors Field, home of the Colorado Rockies baseball team. Also contained in the stadium is The Blue Moon Brewing Company @ the Sandlot, which is where Blue Moon was invented and where the four employees spend most of their time making one-off beers for their patrons to enjoy. Keep in mind, with the exception of special events the stadium is only open during the baseball season, as is the brewery and tours are only available during this time unless a group or private tour is arranged. It's a perfect stop on the way to or from "The Pec."

16th Street Mall

www.16thsteetmalldenver.com

1001 16th St. Denver, CO 80265 (720) 282-9610 (shop, gallery and restaurant hours vary).

Less than a mile from El Chapultepec and itself over a mile long, sits the 16th Street Mall. Featuring a long list of galleries, shops, restaurants, bars, clubs, street vendors and street performers, it has become Denver's version of Venice Beach, though not quite as hipster and a little more mainstream. It's worth a visit if for nothing else than its extensive bar and food choices as well as some outstanding street performers.

Coors Brewery

www.millercoors.com

13th Street Golden, CO 80401 (303) 277-2337 (Thursday-Monday 10am-4pm, Sunday 12pm-4pm, hours differ slightly during the summer).

A short, 20-minute drive from "The Pec" will deliver you into Golden Colorado, and more importantly the Coors brewery. With daily self-paced tours of the world's largest single-site brewery that concludes with free samples of Coors products, this is about as good as tours get. And considering the relationship between The Pec and Coors, it's pretty fitting as well.

BUCKHORN EXCHANGE

DENVER, CO

1000 Osage Street
Denver, CO 80204
(303) 534-9505
http://www.buckhorn.com
http://youtu.be/lniCr3CBZiY

Food: Yes
Live Music: Yes
Hours: Monday—Thursday 11am-9pm, Friday 11am-10pm, Saturday—Sunday 5pm-10pm
Type of Bar: Saloon
What to Drink: Buffalo Bill Cody Cocktail
Why You Should Go: Western saloon with colorful history including Teddy Roosevelt (always fun), and great Western lore.

We must warn you, if you're a member of PETA, an animal lover or anti-hunting advocate, then the Buckhorn Exchange is not the place for you. The founder of this 130-year old saloon was an avid hunter, and his trophies are all displayed throughout the two stories of the Buckhorn Exchange.

THE HISTORY

The Buckhorn Exchange was founded by Henry H. Zeitz in 1893. Zeitz's life reads more like a novel than that of a real person and so, to truly understand the Buckhorn Exchange you must take look at Zeitz's life.

In semi-chronological order, the story goes like this: he hitch-hiked out West at the ripe old age of 10, met the great Indian chief Sitting Bull (look up the story of General Custer if you don't know who that is), became a scout for and close personal friend of Buffalo Bill (who gave him the nick name Shorty Scout), was a bodyguard for Horace Tabor in the silver mining town of Leadville, Colorado (Tabor was also known as the Silver King during that time), founded the Buckhorn Exchange, guided President Teddy Roosevelt on hunts in Colorado and then later hunted with Teddy in Africa.

Henry got his start in the bar business when the US switched from the Gold to Silver standard late in the 19th century. With the switch, Zeitz decided to head back down to Denver from Leadville because his father had started a saloon in the downtown area. A common complaint Zeitz heard from railroad workers was that there was nowhere near work or home to drink. Henry, recognizing an opportunity, purchased the Niff's breweries office and warehouse located across from the rail yard. He then moved the family saloon into the building and, seeing yet another opportunity, offered to cash the rail workers checks on payday. The one catch to cashing the check at the Exchange was that the workers only received part of their checks. A percentage was saved for the wives to pick up later that day for use in the Exchange to purchase food and supplies.

TODAY

Though the focal point used to be the saloon, today the Buckhorn Exchange has become more of a restaurant than a bar. With featured foods like rattlesnake, alligator tail, 64 ounce steaks and Rocky Mountain oysters, the Exchange has become a legend in the Denver culinary scene. But the Buckhorn was founded as, and still is, a bar at its core. If you head upstairs you will find a white oak bar that has played host to Buffalo Bill Cody and President Theodore Roosevelt and that has a story almost as interesting as Henry Zietz himself.

It was hand carved for the Zeitz family for their original saloon in Germany in 1856. When they immigrated to the US they brought the bar by boat to New York, moved it from New York to the Great Lakes via the Eerie Canal, the Great Lakes to Prairie Deshane by rail and then made the final leg of its journey to Denver in 1871 by oxcart.

The décor of the Buffalo Exchange is, to put it mildly, a study in taxidermy. Zeitz's life was full of excitement and adventure,

and the walls certainly reflect it, with mountain lions and mounted deer peering over cases as you munch on a buffalo steak. You'll also see Zeitz's extensive gun collection, an array of Native American artwork he often accepted as payment and even an elk dork (which he'd use to tame rowdy customers).

Be sure to look behind the bar for Colorado liquor license #1, the very first issued after Prohibition.

THE FOOD

As already mentioned, the Buckhorn Exchange specializes in fine cuisine, especially dishes featuring game such as alligator or even rattlesnake. They are most well-known though, as the place in Denver to get a great platter of Rocky Mountain oysters.

Now, if you're not familiar with them, Rocky Mountain

oysters are bull testicles, sliced thin, battered and deep-fried. They have a…unique taste. And for certain they're probably the most unique of bar foods that you'll find anywhere. Try them with cocktail sauce and you probably should have a drink handy.

THE DRINKS

Speaking of drink, the Buckhorn Exchange specializes in a multitude of drinks in their full-service bar but the one we recommend as a must-try is none other than Buffalo Bill's drink of choice, and later named in his honor, the Buffalo Bill Cocktail.

According to oral history—provided by the manager—Cody was told by his doctor to limit his alcohol to one drink per night. So, when down from Golden, he'd stop in at Zeitz's saloon and sip a tall glass of rye whiskey and apple cider on the rocks. This

drink is still served here, though they've substituted bourbon for the rye and apple juice for the cider. It's a refreshing drink, not sweet, with a heavy taste of the whiskey. It's easy to see what Buffalo Bill liked about it.

http://youtu.be/HtP2U89HL9c

NEARBY DISTRACTIONS

Mile High Stadium

www.sportsauthorityfieldatmilehigh.com

1701 Bryant St. Denver, CO 80204,(720) 258-3333 (operating hours vary by game times and event, call or check their website).

Home of the Denver Broncos and a mere two miles from the Buckhorn Exchange sits Sports Authority Field at Mile High or simply Mile High as it is called by most locals. Containing the Colorado Sports Hall of Fame and available for tours, both occur year-round with varying hours, this is a must-see for any Denver Broncos fan.

Ft. Collins

Located approximately one hour north of Denver sits the sleepy town of Ft. Collins, Colorado.

Home of Colorado State University, HP and what is probably the heaviest concentration of world-class breweries in the US.

If you have the time (and a designated driver wouldn't be a bad idea either) head up and check out the free tours at Anheuser-Busch, Odell, New Belgium, Ft. Collins and Equinox to name just a few. Most tours end with free samples or low-priced samples, and touring them all can easily take up an afternoon ending with anyone over 21 feeling pretty good or not good at all, depending on your tolerance.

US Mint

www.usmint.gov

320 West Colfax Avenue Denver, CO 80204 (303) 405-4761 (tours run 8am-11am and 1pm to 4pm).

Less than two miles from the Buckhorn is one of the United States Mints. Producing over 50 million coins per day, the mint offers free daily tours, which must be scheduled in advance via their website and can be scheduled as much as three months in advance. The tour gives you a glimpse into how dull, blank scrap metal slugs (gone are the days of actual metal worth something) are turned into shiny pocket change used to tip the lousy bartenders in saloons not in this book.

OTHER NOTABLE AREA BARS

Buffalo Rose
119 Washington Street, Golden (303) 278-6800
(Monday-Sunday 11am-2am).

One of the oldest bars in the area and, according to them, the oldest in all of Colorado (established in 1858). This is a saloon-turned-dive that caters to live music acts, primarily loud rock. The food is cheap and so are the drinks. We've heard good things about the burgers, but this is only hearsay. At the very least this will give you an excuse to get out of Denver and check out Golden.

Ship Tavern-Brown Palace Hotel
321 17th Street, downtown Denver (303) 297-3111
(Bar Monday-Sunday 11am-12am).

This bar was opened in 1934 after the repeal of Prohibition. It was designed to resemble a waterfront tavern you might find in New England in the 19th century, with gleaming brass, polished wood and antique nautical décor. It's the polar opposite of the Buffalo Rose, with nary a dive bar qualifier (like Christmas tree lights or stale beer smell) to be had. But that being said, the Brown Palace itself is a great place to have a drink in anyway. It was opened in 1892 and at one time had a pretty wild saloon, catering to many of the ne'er-do-wells as one of the less reputable joints in the area.

TUCSON AREA

Tucson, Arizona and its surrounding area are chock full of some of the best and wildest history in the United States. It was in this desert that Wyatt Earp tracked down the rival "Cowboys" gang and took revenge for his brother's murder. It was in this desert that people lost their lives for little more than an insult.

Tucson and nearby Tombstone were dynamic places and are pretty emblematic of what many think of when they think of the Old West. And for good reason: much of what they think is probably true.

Tucson grew up though, even while Tombstone threatened to fade away. Luckily, they kept their history and the uniqueness that makes them so special.

Tucson features a great entertainment scene with an abundance of distractions to keep you busy. Aside from the Bucket List Bars™ in this book, there is 4th Avenue, next to the University of Arizona and teeming with nightlife. Weekend nights there can be a lot of fun, but be careful because it might also get dangerous.

Speaking of danger, Tombstone thrived on it. People lost

their lives on a daily basis in this small town. Every sin and vice to be had in the late 1800s could be had on her streets and in her saloons.

Unlike Tucson, Tombstone didn't grow. Instead it almost passed into obscurity. Had it not been for the tourist industry the town "too tough to die" would have, in fact, died. But luckily much of what was there in the late 1800s is still there today. This goes for both the bars and the spirit. If you can muscle past the tourist-trap feel of this place, there's a great bunch of locals to get to know.

TRANSPORTATION: In Tucson, Orange Cab Company of Tucson (520) 884-7900 (Monday-Sunday 24hrs). Yellow Cab Tucson (520) 624-6611 (Monday-Sunday 5am-8pm). Tombstone does not have a taxi service. The best bet is to stay a night or two in this town and definitely don't drive.

THE BUFFET BAR & CROCKPOT

TUCSON, AZ

538 E. 9th St.
Tucson, AZ, 85705
(520) 623-6811
http://www.thebuffetbar.com
http://youtu.be/mDJwxsGkVpE

Food: Yes
Live Music: No
Hours: Monday—Saturday 6am-2am, Sunday 11am-2am
Type of Bar: Dive
What to Drink: Maker's Mark or Stoli on ice,
Coors Banquet Beer
Why You Should Go: Oldest post-Prohibition dive in
Tucson, friendly hospitality, drink specials.

There are few dark, stale dive bars you can walk into and feel instantly at home. That's the feeling the Buffet gives visitors. Whether it's the friendly staff, the family-like camaraderie of the patrons or the no-nonsense drinking, the Buffet is one of the best bars in America.

THE HISTORY

Located in the Ironhorse District of Old Town Tucson, the Buffet Bar and Crock Pot is Tucson's oldest watering hole. The building was built in 1929 and it actually began serving alcohol in 1934 under the name The Lantern Bar.

The area is known as the Ironhorse District because it's geographically within one mile of the original Tucson train depot. During the early 20th century, railroad workers had to live within a mile of the train depot in order to hear the whistles of arriving trains (and trains in that period were, of course, known as *ironhorses*), hence the name Ironhorse District. It's composed mainly

of single-room bungalows that originally housed the rail road workers and their families.

The Buffet has been continually serving the Tucson community for over 77 years and is not only the premier dive bar of Tucson, but arguably one of the premier dive bars of the whole United States.

TODAY

Today the Buffet is one of the most welcoming bars we've been to and has taken the term dive bar to new (ahem) heights. It was recently featured in Esquire Magazine's "Best Bars in America" section, which said the hot dogs "should never be consumed sober." We did and survived.

Likewise, the Tucson Weekly asked, "...where else but the

Buffet can you order a beer and study the weird mix of college kids, drunks, and the potentially mentally ill? Ah, paradise!" To many the Buffet is just that...paradise.

The décor could be considered eccentric—if graffiti was décor. You'll notice the darkness (standard for a good dive) and the walls covered in magic marker and paint. It's a combination of names, philosophical references, quotes and pictures—and it all kind of runs together in some kind of perfect, Berlin Wall-esque pattern. We were told it's painted over about once a year to be filled up again.

You'll also notice the great decoupage of artifacts from the years scattered about. Most are pretty meaningful so feel free to ask. They also have cheap pool and even cheaper shuffleboard.

The Buffet opens at 6 am daily (except on Sundays when they sleep in until 11 am) and doesn't close until 2 am. While it seems a bit superfluous to open at 6 am, the bar actually caters to those working night shifts, who are just getting off work when the place opens. We're told in the mornings the bar is crowded with delivery people, healthcare workers from the local hospitals and others who work the graveyard shift.

The Buffet has regularly low prices, so they don't offer a happy hour. They do, however, offer a happy minute (two to be exact at 6pm and 11pm). During the 6pm happy minute you get a two-for-one drink deal, you call it. The 11pm happy minute gets you a fresh drink of whatever you have in front of you for one dollar more. Regardless of what it is you're drinking, it's only a buck.

THE FOOD

They're also known for their bar food, specifically their hot dogs, quarter pound polish sausages and pickled eggs. The hot dogs and polish sausages are steamed in beer and served with a huge tray of fixings. The pickled eggs (died red in beet juice) are made with the original owner's recipe. Esquire says you shouldn't eat this stuff sober. We can't say we agree, but if you drink here like you should, then you probably won't be sober when you do try them anyway.

THE DRINKS

They're primarily known for three drinks. First, they have sold more Coors Banquet Beer on tap than any other bar in Arizona.

So much of it, in fact, they were presented a plaque in 1996 from Coors thanking them for selling over 500,000 gallons. Today a 16 ounce glass of draft Coors will run you $2 (yes, you read that right).

Their second and third signature drinks are shots of Makers Mark (they sell more than any other bar in Arizona) and Stoli vodka. For $3.50 you get a 1 ½ ounce shot over ice. It's that easy.

NEARBY DISTRACTIONS

Frog & Firkin
www.frogandfirkin.com
874 East University Blvd., Tucson, AZ 85719, (520) 623-7507
(Sunday-Thursday 11am-1am, Friday-Saturday 11am-2am).

Not in the mood for pickled eggs or brats? Then head on over to Frog & Firken, which is less than a mile away from The Buffet. Featuring some of the best Chicago deep dish style pizzas in Tucson and some outstanding domestic, micro and imported draughts and bottles. It's sure to help you soak up some Stoli and Maker's Mark. Check their website for upcoming events and nifty coupons.

Kino Veteran Memorial Stadium/MLB Spring Training
www.kinosportscomplex.com
2500 E. Ajo Way, Tucson, AZ 85713 (520) 434-1343
(Game/Event time vary).

Tucson plays host to a multitude of Major League Baseball teams for their yearly spring training. Most games occur at the Kino Veteran Memorial Stadium, less than 5 miles from The Buffet and offers attendees a chance to watch some of their favorite teams and players get ready for the upcoming season. Not spring training during your trip? That's ok, the stadium also plays host to the Tucson Padres minor league team.

KON TIKI
TUCSON, AZ

4625 E. Broadway Blvd.
Tucson, AZ, 85711
(520) 323-7193
http://www.kontikitucson.com
http://youtu.be/OprpvwfS-n8

Food: Yes
Live Music: Yes
Hours: Monday—Thursday 11:30am-1:30am, Friday—Saturday 10am-2am, Sunday 10am-12am
Type of Bar: Tiki bar
What to Drink: Scorpion Bowl
Why You Should Go: Classic 1960s Tiki bar in the middle of the desert, great classic drinks, original hand-carved Tikis.

In a fairly humble strip mall in Tucson, Arizona, Kon Tiki demonstrates the style and elegance of the Tiki-bar craze of the mid-20th century. Jutting up from surrounding palm trees and nameless offices and shops is the colorful Tiki mask beckoning visitors to a South Seas tropical escape.

THE HISTORY

Kon Tiki was started at the height of the Tiki bar phenomenon in 1963 by a couple of Tucson's leading restaurateurs: Dean Short and Tom Chandler.

Many of the Tiki bars around the country at that time were part of a chain called Kon Tiki and therefore very similar in appearance, food and drinks. But the owners of *this* Kon Tiki wanted something unique and so they brought in designers from all over the country to make their place stand out from the rest. Everything inside the bar, from the fountains to the Tikis, is custom and one-of-a-kind made specifically for Kon Tiki.

As a matter of fact, the Tikis themselves were made by renowned Tiki carver Milan Guanko who hand-carved each, making them unique in both their style and representation. Kon Tiki has over 20 of the Guanko Tikis, more than any other location in the entire United States.

As Tiki bars declined in popularity in the 70s and 80s so did Kon Tiki. The bar changed ownership multiple times throughout the years and fell into disrepair and neglect and was finally forced to close its doors in 1993. Then current owner Paul

Christopher—originally a dishwasher at Kon Tiki at 14 years old—bought the bar, cleaned it up and reopened it in 1994.

TODAY

With the reopening of the bar by Christopher in 1994, Kon Tiki became a fixture in Tucson and in the worldwide Tiki Bar community. Upon arriving, you will be greeted by Kon Tiki's mantra, "Welcome to Paradise," right above the front door. And as you step into the bar be prepared to be transported to a new world. Though it may be a blazing 105 degrees and bright outside, the first two things you will notice when stepping in is that it is cool (thankfully) and that it's dark. Not dark in the sense that you can't see anything, dark in the sense that you have no idea what time of day it is, what season it is or if the apocalypse is going on outside. The glow of the lights, the sound of the fountains, the Tikis and the Polynesian décor all combine to disconnect you from the real world when you step in.

This feeling of being swept away to somewhere new and different is the perfect example of how a Tiki bar is supposed to make you feel—like a Vegas casino: that's what they're designed for. And to be honest, Kon Tiki is one of the best at it.

People travel from all over the world to visit Kon Tiki and they regularly get visitors from Australia, England, China, Japan, Brazil, Argentina and Canada to name a few.

THE FOOD

Kon Tiki has a full-service kitchen with Polynesian-fusion cuisine. Much of it is in the form of tapas or finger foods, like their

Monkey on a Stick: skewers of marinated beef (the marinade, called volcano sauce, is like the Scorpion Bowl mix in that it is a closely guarded secret), and is served on a bed of rice. They have two kinds: spicy and regular (go with the spicy).

THE DRINKS

Without a doubt you must try Kon Tiki's signature, Scorpion Bowl. Like most Tiki bars, they keep their recipe secret so we don't know exactly what's in the mix, but we can tell you there's no hint of alcohol at all. Because of the large amount of alcohol contained in just one Scorpion Bowl, it can't be served to just a single person (you need a partner in crime to enjoy the whole thing....perfect for a date). Don't despair if you are flying solo though, you can still try the mini scorpion, a single serving of the Scorpion Bowl with the same great taste, just a smaller quantity of alcohol.

Related to the drinks are the mugs that Kon Tiki occasionally has made for them by renowned Tiki artists, Tiki Farm. Each series is limited and one of a kind, no two series are the same, and each is based on one of the Tikis actually at the bar.

http://youtu.be/pNvHWur7PMI

NEARBY DISTRACTIONS

Pima Air & Space Museum

www.pimaair.org

6000 East Valencia Rd. Tucson, AZ 85756 (520) 574-0462 (520) 574-9238 (Open 9 am – 5 pm daily except Thanksgiving and Christmas)

Though it is a bit of a drive (10 miles from Kon Tiki) the Pima Air and Space Museum is worth the trip. Featuring over 300 different aircraft from the US and all over the globe. It is one of the largest Air and Space museums in the world (and the largest not funded by the government). Taking up over 80 acres, it is easy to spend an afternoon marveling at some of mankind's greatest aircraft.

Trail Dust Town

traildusttown.com

6541 East Tanque Verde Road #22 Tucson, AZ 85715 (520) 296-4551 (times vary by attraction, call or visit their website).

Less than 5 miles from Kon Tiki sits Trail Dust Town. This Old West themed attraction features the Pinnacle Peak Steakhouse, one of the most popular steakhouses in Tucson, a Wild West themed stunt show, rides, shooting gallery, shops and the Museum of the Horse Soldier. Most attractions are open until 8 pm or later so you may want to plan your visit after the hottest hours of the day during the summer.

THE TAP ROOM
TUCSON, AZ

311 E. Congress St.
Tucson, AZ 85701
(520) 622-8848
http://www.hotelcongress.com/club/the-tap-room/
http://youtu.be/AwzK8j93fAM

Food: Yes
Live Music: Yes
Hours: Monday—Sunday, 11am-2am
Type of Bar: Pub
What to Drink: Martini or Bloody Mary
Why You Should Go: John Dillinger captured here, the jukebox, original Pete Martinez artwork.

The Tap Room at the Hotel Congress in Tucson, Arizona, has seen more than its fair share of characters pass through its doors, from world-famous artists to actors and rock stars. This is place is a unique, beautiful and worthwhile stop in your nationwide pub-crawl.

THE HISTORY

The Tap Room bar is located in probably one of the most notorious hotels in Tucson's history, the Hotel Congress. The hotel was opened in 1919 and sits directly across from the Tucson railroad station where thousands of travelers passed through on their journey to the Southwest from all over the world. Two of the most notorious area visitors were John Dillinger and Wyatt Earp.

Wyatt shot and killed Frank C. Stilwell in the Tucson rail yard during a shootout that is believed to have been committed in revenge for the killing of Wyatt's younger brother Morgan. The shootout occurred before the hotel and bar had initially opened but it was the start of a series of events that put not only the towns of Tucson and Tombstone on the map, but also the Hotel Congress and the bar it houses.

The bar and hotel were built to serve the area's growing agricultural industry and the railroad passengers arriving in or passing through Tucson. Its location was a perfect stop for travelers since it was a short walk from the station and had all the required services any weary traveler needed: a bed, a restaurant and a bar. Though the train station achieved notoriety for Earp's killing of Stillwell, the hotel and bar existed quietly until January 22, 1934.

On that fateful day, a fire started in the basement under mysterious circumstances and quickly spread to the third floor via the elevator shaft. Staying at the hotel at the time was the gang of bank robber John Dillinger. The group escaped unharmed via exterior fire escapes but left their suitcases behind. Once safely out of the hotel, they bribed a couple of firemen to go back into the hotel and retrieve the gang's luggage containing guns and more than $20,000 in stolen cash.

One of the firemen later recognized the gang members and notified authorities. In the course of hours the small Tucson police force was able to round up the entire Dillinger gang, including John himself, without firing a single shot. When captured, John Dillinger is quoted as simply saying "Well, I'll be damned!"

TODAY

Today the Hotel Congress still stands proudly in downtown Tucson, though one story shorter because of the 1934 fire. Inside, the Tap Room looks like little has changed since its opening in 1933. Visitors find themselves surrounded by period neon, a glimmering waist-high wooden bar, art deco mirrors, old movie poster, priceless works of art and a 1940s Wurlitzer jukebox still belting out jams like the day it was installed.

Much of the art work was created by world-famous painter, rodeo clown and Tap Room regular Pete Martinez. Though they regularly get offers from art collectors and galleries from around the world for the classic paintings, they refuse to sell them, saying Pete's art work belongs in the place he felt most at home.

If you're here towards the end of January, try to catch Dillinger Days, a celebration to honor Tucson's police force, and to remember the capture of John Dillinger and his era. Events include a 1930s-themed gala featuring a street festival, re-enactments from the time period (including the capture of Dillinger), classic cars, music, tours, lectures and much more.

Regardless of when you're here, keep your eye out for the celebrities who frequent the Tap Room. While visiting we ran into Joey Burns, front man for the alt-country band Calexico. And we're told that ZZ Top's Billy Gibbons calls this place his favorite bar.

And, like many old places, the Hotel Congress may be

haunted. According to whispered rumors there is a ghost in a grey suit by the name of T.S., who many have seen peering out of windows on the second floor. Another rumored ghost is that of a woman dressed in a Victorian dress who has been seen smelling the roses in the stairwell and lobby.

But creepiest of all is the rumored goings' on in rooms around the hotel, none more feared or active than the ghost that inhabits room 242, considered the most haunted room in the hotel. Stay here after a having a few drinks downstairs in the bar.

THE FOOD

Hotel Congress features a café (the Cup Café) with offerings throughout the day. They claim an eclectic menu and feature regional fare like huevos rancheros as well as more ethnic cuisine, like Asian-fusion dishes.

THE DRINKS

The Tap Room itself is a full bar. They are renowned for the Bloody Mary and the martini. In fact, local papers have often claimed this to be the best place in the area for sipping a dry martini. No doubt the atmosphere really helps—you can sit at a gleaming Formica countertop listening to Frank Sinatra sing his lungs out on the Wurlitzer behind you while pondering how many olives it really takes to make the drink perfect. Not a bad way to spend an evening.

NEARBY DISTRACTIONS

Southern Arizona Transportation Museum
www.tucsonhistoricdepot.org
**414 N. Toole Ave. Tucson, AZ 85701 (520) 623-2223
(Tuesday-Thursday 11am-3pm, Friday-Saturday 10am-4pm,
Sunday 11am-3pm).**

Located directly across the street from The Tap Room, the Southern Arizona Transportation Museum focuses on the history of Arizona's railroads. But one of its most interesting ties to history is in the form of Wyatt Earp, Doc Holliday and the Cochise County War. It was at this very station that the Earp family, escorted by Wyatt, Doc and others, was preparing to leave from the area when Wyatt spotted and eventually shot Frank Stillwell for his alleged involvement in Morgan Earp's murder. Today the event has been immortalized both in movies and with a statue of Wyatt Earp and Doc Holliday.

The Rialto Theatre

www.rialtotheatre.com

318 E. Congress St. Tucson, AZ 85701 (520) 740-1000
(operating hours vary by show).

Literally right across the street from The Tap Room/Hotel
Congress sits the Rialto Theatre. Opened in 1920 and featuring mainly vaudeville—dance, singing, bands, comedy—performances The Rialto Theatre has withstood the test of time.
Today it features a wide range of acts, from music and comedy,
to lectures and plays. It is a popular destination for locals and
tourists alike.

THE CRYSTAL PALACE

TOMBSTONE, AZ

436 E. Allen St.
Tombstone, AZ, 85638
(520) 457-3611
http://www.crystalpalacesaloon.com
http://youtu.be/pCCAjlH-bws

Food: Yes
Live Music: Yes
Hours: Monday—Sunday 11am-1am
Type of Bar: Saloon
What to Drink: Old Overholt Rye Whiskey
Why You Should Go: Classic American saloon from the Old West, restored almost to original, waiters and waitresses in period dress, gunfight reenactments.

The Crystal Palace is located in the hot and dusty mining town turned tourist destination of Tombstone, Arizona, and has a history more checkered than the Earp brothers or the cowboys they rode against in the 1880s.

HISTORY

The bar began life as the Golden Eagle Brewery on the corner of Fifth Street and Allen Street, which was to become known as one of the bloodiest street corners in the Wild West. Close to midnight on December 28th, 1881, Virgil Earp was walking to the bar when multiple shotgun blasts struck him. Virgil survived but lost the use of his left arm.

Earlier that year, on June 22, a huge fire broke out in Tombstone which wiped out almost the entire town. One of the few surviving buildings was the brewery and bar due to the dedicated work of a bucket brigade (an example of the priorities of the time). Less than a year later, on May 26th of 1882, another fire broke out and an even more valiant effort by the bucket brigade couldn't save the doomed building. Swift action by the town's people saw to it that the establishment was rebuilt quickly, at which time it took on the new name, Crystal Palace, and a whole new personification.

After being rebuilt the Crystal Palace became THE destination for fine dining and entertainment by stage coach passengers making the journey to San Francisco. It was said to feature oysters and other delicacies (though we're still trying to figure out how they got oysters out in the middle of the desert during the 1880s), and a fountain that the Tombstone Epitaph said "spouts forth streams of pure water." The saloon also featured gambling, including faro and wheel of fortune, and some of the finest wines and hard liquor available anywhere in the US at the time. Upstairs it housed the offices of Virgil Earp (Wyatt's older brother) and Dr. Goodfellow (portrayed in the movie, "Tombstone" as the doctor pulling bullets out of Wyatt's younger brother Morgan when he died).

TODAY

Over the years the bar has opened and closed numerous times, has served multiple roles including a movie theater and a greyhound bus station, gone through a rash of owners, and even sold all of its gambling tables and the original bar to a bar in Naco,

Mexico during Prohibition (unfortunately the original bar perished in a fire). Though the Crystal Palace has had a rough life it was eventually bought and restored by owner Kimmie and today is a cornerstone in both the town and the experience of Tombstone.

The miners, cowboys, outlaws, gunfighters and prostitutes, of yesterday have long since left the building (so to speak) only to be replaced by fake bullets, tourists and a hand full of locals. That's not to say the bar has lost any of its appeal though. The current owner, along with her son, R.J., have done their best to make the Crystal Palace feel much like it did in the 19th century, both in the physical makeup (there are still original bullet holes in the ceiling, a fake second story and many of the original fixtures) and the authentic costumes of the waitresses and bartenders. Adding to the authenticity are actors dressed as gun-slinging cowboys who regularly act out historic gunfights both in and outside of the bar.

THE FOOD

Gone are the oysters (and we must reiterate our dubiousness at their claim of freshness in the middle of the Arizona desert in 1886) as well as the other attempts to woo the crowds on their way to San Francisco. Here you find simple bar-menu fixings, like their burgers, fries and sandwiches. However, they're known for their smoked barbeque ribs. We'll suggest this at the passed-on suggestion from the cook, R.J., who swears by them (but then, of course, he's the one that makes them…).

THE DRINKS

At the Crystal Palace you really must try the Old Overholt rye whiskey. Old Overholt was originally distilled in Broad Ford, Pennsylvania and claims to have been founded in 1810. Today it is a subsidiary of Jim Beam and is distilled in Clermont, Kentucky. Regardless of the change of venue or ownership, it's the oldest whiskey brand in the United States. What makes the drink even more special is that it was Doc Holliday's drink of choice. In the 1880s, he would regularly sit at the Crystal Palace sipping a bit of Old Overholt while playing cards. We can't think of a more fitting drink in a place like this.

http://youtu.be/vazhcBacVAc

NEARBY DISTRACTIONS

The Bird Cage Theatre
www.tombstonebirdcage.com
535 East Allen St. Tombstone, AZ 85638 (520) 457-3421 (Monday-Sunday 8am-6pm).

A mere 341 feet from the Crystal Palace, The Bird Cage Theatre is a must see for any visitor to the area. Once known as the wildest and wickedest night spot on the western frontier, it featured varying kinds of shows, prostitutes and gambling. Believed to have been the scene of at least 26 murders and containing over 100 bullet holes, it's a rare and unique look into life as it was during one of America's most storied chapters. Be forewarned though, guests and employees alike claim to see ghosts on a regular basis.

Boothill Graveyard
www.tombstonechamber.com/Boothill-Graveyard
408 N. Hwy 80 Tombstone, AZ 85638 (520) 457-3300 (Monday-Sunday 730am- Dusk).

Probably one of the most notorious graveyards in the entire US, it features some of the most well-known and even humorous gravestone inscriptions. Does "Here lies Lester Moore, four slugs from a 44, no Les, no More" sound familiar? You'll find this as well as gravestones evidencing the infamous Earp and Cowboys war throughout the graveyard. Best of all, it is one of the few free attractions still available today.

The "Good Enough Mine" Underground Tour
www.tombstonechamber.com
The Good Enough Mine Underground Tour, 5th & Toughnut St.
Tombstone, AZ 85638 (520) 255-5553 (open daily, call for hours).

Discovered by Tombstone founder Ed Schieffelin, the "Good Enough Mine" was one of the initial mines responsible for causing the silver rush that helped to turn Tombstone into a boom town. Informative and fun, the tour features a glimpse into mining in the 1800s including a trip underground to view a small portion of the historic and vast mine.

OTHER NOTABLE AREA BARS

The Shanty
401 East 9th Street Tucson, AZ 85705 (520) 623-2664 (Monday-Sunday 12pm-1am).

Not far from Buffet Bar, The Shanty is Tucson's oldest continuously serving bar, opening right after the repeal of Prohibition. This is definitely a locals' joint, with a healthy mix of college students and young professionals. It's also the only bar in the immediate area with pool tables, so those partying in some of the local clubs like to duck in here to relax for a bit. They serve strong drinks and cold beer, and their bar snack of choice—popcorn—never goes out of style.

Chicago Bar
5954 East Speedway Boulevard Tucson, AZ 85712 (520) 748-8169 (Monday-Sunday 10am-2am).

This live music bar is a favorite of Tucson natives and students alike. They feature live music and cover bands most every night of the week, including some very good local blues bands. A bit divey, but the drinks are cheap and the music is loud.

Big Nose Kate's
417 East Allen Street Tombstone, AZ 85638 (520) 457-3107 (Monday-Sunday 10am-12am).

A short walk down the wooden sidewalk from the Crystal Palace is the other famous saloon in Tombstone, Big Nose Kate's.

Named after Doc Holliday's prostitute girlfriend, it was originally the site of Tombstone's Grand Hotel, a richly appointed hotel where visitors traveling to or from one of the coasts could rest in elegance. The place isn't as authentic as the Crystal Palace (which actually was the Crystal Palace), and it's the quintessential tourist trap, but it's still a fun place to spend a couple of hours drinking.

LAS VEGAS AREA

Really, are there any other cities that come to your mind when you think of having a good time, of drinking your cares away, of relaxing on the other side of a bar from a friendly bartender happy to serve you drinks and listen to your banter? If the answer is "yes, any city *but* Las Vegas," then you're a lot like us.

The truth is, Las Vegas is a terrible bar city. Sure, it has all the nightclubs and lounges you could want, but bars are a different story.

You wouldn't think so, would you? At one time Las Vegas was flush with great places to drink, meet friends and enjoy company. But, all of these places drifted away in favor of other, more trendy spots.

In fact, one of the coolest places in about a 50-mile radius closed up in early 2011. Atomic Liquors, with its famous neon and kitschy décor, started when Las Vegas was exploiting the nearby H-bomb tests, and remained unchanged for over 50 years. Luckily some loyal patrons plan on re-opening it for 2013. But we almost lost it!

Simply put, bars aren't flashy. They don't pull in the money like the $500 bottle-service places do. The celebrities don't go to bars when they go to Vegas, they go to nightclubs. That's where the money is.

And, just to be clear, we did cover one nightclub in this book—Mother's in Chicago—but that place hasn't changed in over 40 years. In Las Vegas? They change the décor, the music, the whole environment like a Kardashian changes her wardrobe.

And for those places that aren't nightclubs, that are actual lounges or bars, most all of them are attached to the casino, and hopes of conversation and peace are usually dashed quicker than our streaks at the blackjack table.

True bar aficionados find a tough time going to Sin City. Where can they go to escape Las Vegas itself (for, that's what a bar is after all, an escape)? Aside from jumping on the next plane and heading home, there are still a couple of options.

TRANSPORTATION: In Las Vegas cabs are plentiful and you'll have no problem getting one. Unlike other cities you don't hail taxis on the street in Las Vegas. Instead you must go to a hotel's taxi stand and wait to be picked up. Going to Goodsprings is a different story altogether, though. One option is to charter a limo to take you out. Most cost about $50 per hour including fuel surcharges (but not tip). You'll need a minimum of three-four hours to make the Pioneer Saloon.

PIONEER SALOON
GOODSPRINGS, NV

310 Spring Street
Goodsprings, NV 89019
(702) 874-9362
http://www.pioneersaloon.info
http://youtu.be/zX0PimkvMSk

Food: Yes
Live Music: No
Hours: Monday—Sunday, 9am-12am
Type of Bar: Saloon
What to Drink: Shot and a beer
Why You Should Go: The real history of the area outside of Las Vegas, great bar with unusual gaming, and just to become a full-fledged Asshole.

This is the history of the Las Vegas area that, chances are, you've never seen. The Pioneer is a good 30 miles from the Strip but worth every mile you log. This authentic, old West saloon has been perfectly preserved in the desert. Yet it's not a tourist trap, more like the neighborhood bar you've been searching for.

HISTORY

The Pioneer Saloon was founded in 1913 by entrepreneur George Fayle, who came to Goodsprings, Nevada because of the boom it was experiencing in the early 1900s. The boom reached its peak in 1910, with everything from lead to zinc and copper being pulled out of the nearby hills.

After World War I, the price for these metals dropped because the demand was simply no longer there. And so, like many towns in the Southwest, Goodsprings just kind of faded away. Many of the buildings were actually relocated to Southern California, and many others just sort of rusted into nothing.

But when Fayle built his saloon to quench the thirst of the local miners, he sought the help of a business that was actually commonly utilized in many of the boom towns in the West: Sears and Roebuck, Inc.

Sears, in the early 1900s, sold just about anything you could think of through its catalogs and that included buildings. In fact it would sell whole houses, delivered to you on the railroad and then constructed at your homestead. In this case though, Fayle purchased a tin building (actually, two of them, including the general store next door). The outside walls of the Pioneer Saloon are stamped tin to look like bricks, and the entire interior (except the floor) is also stamped tin.

You can imagine that with little humidity or wet weather the condition hasn't changed much since the day it was constructed.

And befitting its place in the West, the Pioneer has seen its share of rowdy nights. One such episode put a man—a cheater at cards—six feet under. Apparently the miner had been winning pretty regularly, so often so as to become irregular in fact. When the dealer called him on his streak the gambler lunged at him, prompting the dealer to stick a revolver in the gambler's face and tick off about three rounds. He died on the floor of the saloon. If you look on the wall towards the back of the bar you'll see the sun peeking through three, perfectly round bullet holes.

The Pioneer Saloon is also famous for being the place where

the actor Clark Gable grieved over his wife's death after her airplane crashed into the mountain right behind the bar. He reportedly stayed in the place by himself, drinking for a full day and night while her body was being recovered.

TODAY

The Pioneer Saloon excels at being fun. From the Chicken Shit Bingo to their Asshole club, there isn't a thing about this place that isn't geared towards the smart-ass of the bar aficionados.

Maybe it's because they're so far away from the Strip they have to be as different as possible, or maybe it's just the result of 100 years in the hot sun. Whatever the cause the Pioneer Saloon couldn't be more different than the corporate blandness of the Las Vegas Strip.

When you visit, there are a few things you have to do. The first is to play the aforementioned Chicken Shit Bingo. Essentially the game involves placing a bet on one of many squares painted on the bottom of a small cage. Then a chicken is placed in the cage and whatever square the chicken shits on is the winner. Talk about a game of chance!

The second is to become an Asshole, something that only costs five dollars. Once upon a time the small town council of Goodsprings was seeking toy donations for local charities. When they asked the mayor if he wanted to recruit the regulars of the Pioneer Saloon down the street, he replied that "they're just a bunch of assholes."

The result was a huge toy drive by the regulars, and the

tradition of calling themselves assholes—but with pride. Now, for a small sum you too can be sworn in as an Asshole (and your money still goes to helping out underprivileged kids).

Generally speaking the place simply makes you feel welcome. At the same time it feels like being transported to the Wild West, when dealers still carried guns and popped off cheaters at their tables.

You'll spend an hour to get here, but trust us when we tell you it's worth it.

THE FOOD

In the next door General Store they have a kitchen that serves up basic pub grub: burger, fries and such. But, the really cool part about the place is the back patio lined with gas grills.

For no charge you can bring your own steak, burger, hot dogs or anything else you can imagine and grill your own food for free. Almost like bringing your own booze to a restaurant, but instead you're bringing the food to the booze joint.

So, on your way out of Las Vegas, stop by a grocery store and pick up a couple of steaks to throw on the grill and then enjoy them on the patio.

THE DRINKS

They don't really have a signature drink, though they have a full bar and make all the basics as expected.

It's probably best to stick to the basics, too, considering the history of this joint. Try the simple bottle of beer or (even better) a shot or two of a good American whiskey—something they would have been drinking at the table right *before* the gambler got caught and then, subsequently, plugged.

NEARBY DISTRACTIONS

Gold Strike Hotel & Gambling Hall
www.stopatjean.com
1 S. Main Street Jean, NV 89019 (800) 634-1539
(Monday-Sunday 24hrs).

The Gold Strike Hotel and Gambling Hall is only seven miles from the Pioneer Saloon and one of the few places out in this relatively desolate area. Featuring a hotel and full-service casino it is the perfect place to stop for the night if you have had a little too much to drink, are hungry or just have that gambling itch.

Sloan Canyon National Conservation Area
www.blm.gov/nv
(for directions visit the BLM website).

About 20 minutes from the Pioneer Saloon, and on the way into or out of Las Vegas, is the Sloan Canyon National Conservation Area. Featuring multiple hiking trails, the area's main attractions are its petroglyphs. Believed to have been created by native cultures there are over 300 rock art panels with 1,700 individual designs. A great stop to stretch your legs and enjoy a hike.

OTHER NOTABLE AREA BARS

Fireside Lounge @ Peppermill Las Vegas
2985 South Las Vegas Boulevard Las Vegas, NV 89109
(702) 735-4177 (Monday-Sunday 24hrs)

If you were looking for a filming location to shoot the sleazy past of Las Vegas, this would probably be the first place you'd go. In fact, that's just what directors like Martin Scorsese have done. The place has graced the strip since 1972, and unlike most other places on the same street, they've refused to change. The décor is campy 1970s, which is cool now. The waitresses still wear dresses with slits up to their waists, which again are in style. In other words, this place didn't change, it just waited for the rest of the world to catch up to it. Have a Scorpion Bowl with a partner, and then take a cab to your hotel.

Decatur Tavern
4680 South Decatur Boulevard Las Vegas, NV 89103
(702) 248-5332 (Monday-Sunday 24hrs)

This is a local's bar, one of the last left in the city. It was founded in 1963, making it older than most anything else in the area—especially considering it hasn't had the face-lift that any of the others have had after being around longer than, say, ten years. A lot of the service-oriented professionals from the city come here when they get off, which means that this is the place to go on just about any given night. The specialty drink is cold beer, so be sure to order at least a couple and just enjoy what it must be like to live in the city everybody else in the world wants to travel to.

Four Mile Bar

3650 Boulder Highway Las Vegas, NV 89121 (702) 431-6936 (Monday-Sunday 24hrs).

Opened at some point in the '40s (memories seem to lapse when you ask precise questions), this dive well away from the strip is a combination Cheers and truck stop. It has one of the most loyal followings of regulars we've ever seen and their karaoke is legendary. The beer is phenomenally cold and the service is warm. All in all, this is the type of bar cities are built on.

LOS ANGELES AREA

You know, with such a large city, you'd expect an equally impressive history concerning the city's bars and the drinking in general. And in general, the City of Angels is one of the foremost cities to drink in—there's something for everyone here.

The city's history is tied to the rich Spanish heritage of the area. After all, the first brewery to be built in California was built under Spanish rule.

However, interestingly enough, not much remains of those earliest settlers, at least not where drinking spots are concerned. In L.A. we don't find the 150-year-old saloons like we do in the northern part of the state.

And, oddly enough, we also don't find any evidence of the Spanish linked to the city's bars either. There aren't any cantinas or old watering holes left.

But what we do find is a greatly diverse mix of 20th-century bars that run the gamut from speakeasy to Tiki bar to dive. Los Angeles has one of the best mixtures of bar types, even if they're not as old as what you'd find in perhaps New York or the Washington D.C. area.

If you're going to take the Bucket List Bar™ tour of L.A., take the whole thing. The different styles of bars, the history in and around them, and the different ages that each of them represent make this the best historic pub crawl in the book!

TRANSPORTATION: Before getting into a taxi in Los Angeles, make sure it has the official City of Los Angeles Taxicab Seal. This seal denotes the cab is insured and regulated, and the driver is trained and authorized to drive. Without the seal the car is a "bandit" cab and likely to take advantage of you. To be sure, use one of the following: United Independent Taxi (all except for Tonga Hut) (800) 411-0303 (Monday-Sunday 24hrs). Bell Cab (all except for Tonga Hut) (800) 666-6664 (Monday-Sunday 24hrs). City Cab (Tonga Hut) (800) 750-4400 (Monday-Sunday 24hrs).

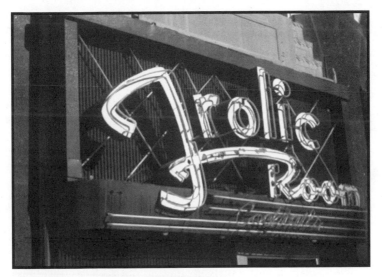

FROLIC ROOM

HOLLYWOOD, CA

6245 Hollywood Boulevard
Los Angeles, CA 90028
(323) 462-5890
http://youtu.be/a9jmCNiTDjQ

Food: No
Live Music: No
Hours: Monday—Sunday 11am-2am
Type of Bar: Dive
What to Drink: A martini or a PBR
Why You Should Go: Last true bar on Hollywood
Boulevard, celebrity sightings, and the Black Dahlia
history.

Located just a few blocks east of Highland Avenue on Hollywood Boulevard, dating back to the 1930s and rumored to have been a speakeasy, the Frolic Room is the last remaining true bar on Hollywood Boulevard. You might even say that the Frolic Room is one of the last "real" things left in Hollywood.

THE HISTORY

There is no concrete evidence that we could find about how the Frolic Room got its start or its name, but the current owner, Robert L. Nunley, gave us his take on how it all started. With that information and a little digging on our own, we think we have come up with a little insight into the Frolic Room and its storied past.

In 1930 the Pantages Theatre was built to host live vaudeville performances as well as first-run movies. At the time of its construction, Prohibition was still in full swing and would be for another three years. As is evidenced by the still remaining stairs and a bricked-in entrance, the area that houses the Frolic Room today was at one time attached to the Pantages Theatre. Many believe this was the only door leading in or out of the Frolic Room. It's rumored that an individual by the name of Freddy Frolic was the host of the room, which he set up so actors, actresses, and distinguished guests would have a place to enjoy a cocktail or two after the show.

Much of this is speculation, but we do know the Frolic Room formally became a bar in 1934, and in 1949, Howard Hughes bought the attached Pantages Theatre. Hughes moved his personal offices into the second floor and the theatre hosted the Academy Awards from 1949 until 1959. More rumors suggest Hughes hosted many private parties in the Frolic Room and we imagine the place saw more than its fair share of famous patrons during that time.

On the other side of all the glitz and glamour of the Frolic Room's past exists a darker and more twisted story. On January 15th, 1947, Elizabeth Short's body was found in the Leimert Park neighborhood, gruesomely mangled, disfigured and cut in half. Elizabeth would come known as the Black Dahlia and the Frolic Room was one of the last places she was ever seen alive. Her murder to this day remains unsolved, though plenty of speculation is provided in books and movies as to who is responsible for the disturbing act. One thing that has remained constant in all the speculation is that the Frolic Room was one of Elizabeth's favorite bars.

During the 1970s and 1980s the Frolic Room and the surrounding area became caught up in the seediness and decay that infected many of America's cities. The area was known more for pimps, hookers, the homeless, drug addicts, and dealers than today's array of restaurants, clubs and boutiques. But the Frolic Room resisted both decay and change as Los Angeles and Hollywood Boulevard evolved into the tourist destination it's become today.

TODAY

Located right in front of Gary Cooper's star on the Walk of Fame, the Frolic Room remains an iconic and original part of storied Hollywood Boulevard. The interior dates back to 1963 when the last remodel was completed. The Al Hirschfeld mural on the wall is likely the only one of its kind and is truly reminiscent of Hollywood's golden age. Befitting its classic status, the bartenders still wear vests and bow-ties, and the bar features a no-nonsense list of cheaply priced and stiffly prepared drinks (an all-time favorite is still the martini).

Gita Bull, longtime bartender at the Frolic Room, said that their crowd depends on what is playing at the theatre next door or at other shows nearby. But, she also told us that "you can be sitting next to a homeless person on one side and Kiefer (Sutherland) on the other."

It will get packed at night, especially on a weekend night, oftentimes by those going to a show, but frequently by regulars. Those regulars, according to Gita, are more the hipster set. But

don't let that detract from wanting to go; it's a piece of Hollywood history that's just too rare to miss.

THE DRINKS

They don't have a signature drink per se at the Frolic Room. They do have a full bar and the bartenders are pretty old-school, so they can mix up just about anything you want.

If you go for a mixed drink, make it something classic. We suggest a martini, just because it seems to go with the era this place is based in.

If you're looking for a beer then go with a PBR; you'll blend in with the skinny-jean-wearing crowd trying to get in the door.

NEARBY DISTRACTIONS

Hollywood Walk Of Fame
www.walkoffame.com

Running east to west on Hollywood Boulevard from North Gower Street to North La Brea, the Hollywood Walk of Fame is 1.3 miles long. That stretch includes the sidewalk in front of the Frolic Room, making a visit to this historic landmark a requirement to get into the bar itself. However, a visit to the Frolic room isn't complete without spending some time walking Hollywood Boulevard viewing the shops, restaurants, interesting characters lining the street and, of course, the Walk of Fame.

Grauman's Chinese Theatre
www.chinesetheatres.com
6801 Hollywood Blvd. Hollywood, CA 90028 (323) 461-3331 (open seven days a week for tours; call ahead as hours change; movie show times vary).

Grauman's Chinese Theatre is an iconic landmark along Hollywood Boulevard and one that almost anyone would recognize though few could tell you its name. Opened in 1927, the theatre cost $2,000,000 to build and even today it is often considered the most lavish and sought-after theatre in Hollywood for studio premieres. It also features nearly 200 celebrity footprints and autographs scribed into the concrete at the theatre's entrance. Less than a mile from the Frolic Room, it's a must-see during your walk along Hollywood Boulevard.

Pantages Theater

www.broadwayla.org

6233 Hollywood Blvd. Los Angeles, CA 90028, (323) 468-1770 (operating hours vary by show).

Literally connected to the Frolic Room, the Pantages Theatre opened in 1930 and was built to host vaudeville performances and first-run movies. Throughout its years it's had multiple owners, including Howard Hughes, and even hosted the annual Academy Award ceremonies. Today it's one of L.A.'s leading venues for live performances and a great place to catch a show before, after, or in between visits to the Frolic Room.

Hollywood Bowl

www.hollywoodbowl.com

2301 North Highland Avenue Los Angeles, CA 90068 (323) 850-2000, (operating hours vary by season and show).

Built in 1919, the Hollywood Bowl is the world's largest natural amphitheater and has played host to a long list of world-famous symphonies, operas, ballets, presidential addresses and concerts. Today it continues the same tradition of summertime events enjoyed under a starlit sky with most people arriving early to enjoy a picnic with family and friends (you can bring your own picnic basket or even arrange to have one waiting for you). With ticket prices sometimes as low as $1, the Hollywood Bowl is definitely worth looking into during your trip to the area.

TOWNHOUSE (DEL MONTE SPEAKEASY)

VENICE, CA

52 Windward Avenue
Venice, California 90291
310-392-4040
http://townhousevenice.com/
http://youtu.be/7FrRpjtDrgA

Food: No
Live Music: Yes
Hours: Monday—Thursday 5pm-2am,
Friday—Sunday 12pm-2am
Type of Bar: Speakeasy
What to Drink: Manhattan
Why You Should Go: The speakeasy downstairs, the feeling of drinking in a 1920s saloon, and the craft cocktails.

Described as "Los Angeles's oldest and most venerable watering hole," the Townhouse in Venice, California, is a prime example of how a bar can come so very close to perfection.

THE HISTORY

Originally opened in 1915 by Italian immigrant Cesar Menotti, the Townhouse is the oldest continuously operating bar in the Los Angeles area. At the time of its opening it was called Menotti's Buffet, and Venice Beach was a very different place than the veritable commune of hipsters, artists, street performers and bums it is today.

In 1915, Venice Beach had luxury hotels, an elegant promenade, plans for an opera house and the Abbot Kinney Pier. The Pier, larger and more extravagant than the current Santa Monica pier, was located at the end of the same street the Townhouse is located on today and contained an amusement park, an aquarium, a hotel, restaurants and a grand dance hall.

Overnight, Prohibition changed the face of Venice, California, as many of the elegant hotels had to stop serving. However, it didn't do much to slow down the Townhouse.

Ever the entrepreneur, Cesar Menotti didn't miss a step when he turned his upstairs bar into a grocery and the basement into a chic and popular speakeasy. To get in and out, customers had to be raised and lowered by a small, two-person hand-operated elevator.

Menotti was able to keep his speakeasy well-stocked by using a steam and utilities maintenance tunnel running from the base of the Abbot Kinney Pier to Menotti's place, and then into other parts of the city. Because during Prohibition the territorial waters of the US only extended out three miles, ships would come down from Canada and anchor offshore. Small boats would then ferry the booze from the larger vessels anchored offshore to the base of the pier where it was carried to Menotti's speakeasy (as well as others in the area).

TODAY

When current owner Louie Ryan bought the Townhouse in 2007, he brought in world-famous interior decorator Nathalie Chapple to renovate and redesign the bar and speakeasy with the

goal of bringing the place back to its original luster. Simply put, they were extremely successful.

Today the bar is more traditional yet still decorated with period accents. But it's the downstairs portion—The Del Monte Speakeasy— that is the true gem of the Townhouse. The speakeasy exudes a different atmosphere altogether, with a dress code, small-band music and access to the more sophisticated side of the cocktail culture.

The trip down the stairs into the speakeasy is more like a short journey back in time to the roaring twenties. When you reach the bottom of the stairs you almost expect to look up and see Cesar Menotti sitting at the bar with a drink.

During our visit we were lucky enough to spend time with two fantastic bartenders, Brandon Ristaino and George Czarnecki, both great mixologists and both devoted to their craft.

Brandon is a throw-back to a time when barmen were true artisans. Responsible for the Townhouse's monthly drink rotation, their move to using fresh juices, house-made syrups and hand-cut ice, he is to cocktails what DaVinci was to art.

George, a fixture at the Townhouse for years, can give you all of the history that we left out. A favorite among the patrons, he has a million dollar voice that's perfect for telling the stories of the Townhouse and Venice Beach.

THE DRINKS

If the ambience of the bar itself doesn't make this one of the best saloons you've ever seen, then surely the drinks will make you fall in love with the place. The passion they pour into their period cocktails is both astounding and inspiring. From their devotion to the perfect ice—they use a custom-made, extra dense ice specially created for them—to their custom-blended Buffalo Trace Bourbon, they take the art of making traditional cocktails to a whole new level.

There are two drinks they make here—both whiskey-based—that really should be your selections when you visit. The first is the Old Fashioned, especially if you can have Brandon make it for you.

The second, the one to choose if you're facing George, is the Manhattan.

Both drinks are traditional, period drinks that use the best ingredients they have, from the hand-cut, dense ice to their own whiskey. They are mixed with devotion and effort that most just don't put into their drinks.

http://youtu.be/qhI1IACtsdw

http://youtu.be/71ZlQfRKJIo

NEARBY DISTRACTIONS

Venice Beach

www.venicebeach.com

1800 Ocean Front Walk, Venice, CA 90291 (open all year).

The Townhouse is literally steps away from the Venice Beach Boardwalk, so why not spend some time exploring one of the most unique destinations in Los Angeles, if not the entire planet. The Boardwalk is more of a shop-lined sidewalk than an actual boardwalk and features restaurants, food stands, shops, street vendors and street performers. Be prepared for some unusual sights and sounds, depending on where you're from, as the area continues to wear its tradition of liberal social change as a badge of honor. Though an alien and strange place to most, it's still worth a visit as it will give you a chance to experience a culture available in few, if any, locations in the world.

Santa Monica Pier

www.santamonicapier.org

200 Santa Monica Pier, Santa Monica, CA 90401 (the pier is always open but hours for businesses on the pier vary).

A short three miles up the beach from the Townhouse is the Santa Monica Pier. Built in 1909 it was originally built as a Municipal Pier with a pipeline running under its 1,600-foot length that ran treated sewage out to the ocean, a practice that stopped in the 1920s. Today the pier is a destination for locals and tourists alike featuring an amusement park, restaurants, an aquarium and a bar. Time your visit to watch the breathtaking sunset.

The Proud Bird

www.theproudbird.com

11022 Aviation Blvd. Los Angeles, CA 90045 (310) 670-3093 (Monday-Thursday 11am-9pm, Friday-Saturday 11am-1pm, Sunday 9am-9pm).

A short five mile drive from the Townhouse is the Proud Bird restaurant and bar. Located adjacent to one of America's busiest runways and airports (LAX), it gives diners the unique experience of enjoying a meal in the open air while literally being feet from landing aircraft. Consider it a stop on your way to or from the airport or just as a purely unique dining experience.

TONGA HUT

LOS ANGELES, CA

12808 Victory Blvd.
North Hollywood, CA 91606
(818) 769-0708
http://www.tongahut.com
http://youtu.be/WwRylBIgvoE

Food: No
Live Music: Yes
Hours: Monday—Sunday 4pm-2am
Type of Bar: Tiki
What to Drink: DB Punch or the Rhumboogie
Why You Should Go: Oldest existing (original) Tiki bar
in the L.A. area, great décor, killer drinks, and the Loyal
Order of the Drooling Bastard.

Having opened its doors in 1958, the Tonga Hut claims the title of being L.A.'s oldest Tiki bar still in operation today. Steeped in North Hollywood history, the Tonga Hut pleases new and regular patrons with twists like the Loyal Order of the Drooling Bastard. It is by far one of the best Tiki bars in all of L.A.

THE HISTORY

In 1958, twenty-four years after Don the Beachcomber opened, brothers Ace and Ed Libby opened the Tonga Hut in North Hollywood, CA, inspired by their travels through the South Pacific and the growing popularity of Tiki bars. Ace and Ed found their perfect location and brought in a builder and designer to transform it into a Polynesian oasis. Using no more than a piece of chalk and the floor as his canvas, the designer drew the life-size layout for seating, the front and back bar and decorative concepts. Impressed by the ideas, the brothers gave the go-ahead and the Tonga Hut was born.

After opening, the bar quickly became a staple and a favorite escape for the citizens of the San Fernando Valley. The "Hut," as it was referred to became "The" Tiki bar in North Hollywood throughout the late 1950s and 1960s until Tiki culture fell out of favor sometime in the 1970s (f***ing disco). Through the 1980s and 1990s the bar continued to be a favorite local hang out but the "Tiki" ness slowly faded away. The fountains stopped working and the bar eventually turned into a dive/sports bar featuring TVs, dart boards and plenty of taxidermy.

The current owners took the place over in 2005 and quickly began restoring the Tonga Hut "sports bar" back to the Tonga Hut "Tiki bar."

TODAY

Today the Tonga Hut is owned by Amy Boylan and Jeremy Fleener. Fleener, guitarist for SX-10 (and formerly of Cyprus Hill), originally fell in love with the Tonga Hut upon his initial visit back in the 1990s. They purchased the bar in 2005 and immediately set about restoring it to its original luster. The video games, neon beer signs and sports memorabilia that were a part of the dive/sports bar were immediately torn out and replaced with traditional Tiki décor. This included the repair of long-broken fountains, the reintroduction of Tiki mugs, multiple traditional Tikis and some custom risqué velvet paintings of beautiful island women painted by local artist Jasin Sallin.

When you step out of the bright California sun and into the

Polynesian oasis that is the Tonga Hut, it is immediately apparent that Amy and Jeremy's love for the place and hard work has paid off. The atmosphere is pure island and leaves little to be desired as far as Tiki bars are considered. The décor is simple, the atmosphere relaxed and the liquid aloha flows heavily into some of the finest concoctions. When you stop by simply kick back with a few island-themed drinks (more on those shortly,) listen to some jams on the jukebox, talk with the bartenders, locals and regulars, or spend your time just taking it all in.

And if you find yourself in the Tonga Hut during happy hour you'll notice a "RESERVED" sign on the bar placed there in honor of Dottie. But who is Dottie and why does she have a reserved seat?

Dottie and her husband started coming to the Tonga Hut in 1961 during the heyday of Tiki bars and quickly became regulars, showing up every day of the week (except Sundays, of course). Every day they ordered the same things: Brandy Alexander for Dottie and Scotch and soda for her husband. Dottie's husband passed away in the early '80s, but Dottie continued the tradition and arrived every weekday at 4pm to enjoy happy hour. She continued to order her usual as well as a scotch and soda with a lemon twist and water back in honor of her husband.

Dottie was a staple at the Tonga Hut and it's said she could tell you anything about the place: its customers, owners, and employees. Sadly, in February of 2010 she passed away at 87 years young. In homage to Dottie and her 49-year presence at the Tonga Hut, her very seat and place at the bar is reserved everyday during Happy Hour. Don't try to sit there.

The Tonga Hut also features a rite of sorts called the Loyal Order of the Drooling Bastard.

The Tonga Hut created the Order to commemorate the long lost art of the Tiki cocktail as outlined in the *Grog Log*, a book by Jeff Berry that has become the bible of exotic tropical drinks. Berry spent years immersing himself in Tiki culture while tracking down the founding recipes of Tiki-themed cocktails. His resulting record resurrects the drinks and the craft bar tending that goes into making island-inspired cocktails.

If you choose to accept the challenge of becoming a Bastard, you must finish every cocktail contained in the Grog Log (at your own pace). Once finished you receive your name on the Drooling Bastard plaque and a life-long discount on some of the Tonga Hut's signature drinks.

THE DRINKS

Tiki bars are notorious for their island-themed drinks and the Tonga Hut didn't disappoint. We tried a few and came out with two winners.

First up was the "Rhumboogie," made with Sailor Jerry Spiced Rum, a secret mix of tropical juices and a 151 rum float. This drink packs both great flavor and the one-two punch of Sailor and Bacardi 151. The Tonga Hut says "It'll boogie on your brain!" and we can't agree more.

Second up is the "DB Punch" which contains Appleton Rum, Ginger liqueur, Blood Orange liqueur, and a mixture of juices. Designed specifically for The Loyal Order of the Drooling Bastard, this stuff is dangerously tasty and easy to drink. Perfect for a hot Southern California day to help numb the mind.

http://youtu.be/DXG_IKaClik

NEARBY DISTRACTIONS

Universal Studios

www.universalstudios.com, 100 Universal City Plaza Universal City, CA 91608 (800) 864-8377 (open year round, hours vary by season, check website).

Only six miles away from the Tonga Hut, Universal Studios has become a world-renowned attraction. Featuring some of the all-time greatest show and movie-themed rides as well as the world's largest working movie studio, this place is fun for any age. Keep in mind it is usually busiest over holidays and the summer, making a Front of Line Pass worth the money.

Griffith Observatory

www.griffithobs.org, 2800 East Observatory Road Los Angeles, CA 90027 (213) 473-0800 (Wednesday-Friday 12pm-10pm, Saturday-Sunday 10am-10pm).

Only 12 miles from the Tonga Hut is one of the most famous and visited landmarks in southern California: the Griffith Observatory. The observatory features public events almost daily, like the L.A. Astronomical Society's Public Star Party, and has been featured as a backdrop in a long list of movies and shows. Admission is free to the Observatory building and grounds but there is a nominal charge to see shows located in the Samuel Oschin Planetarium.

Hollywood Sign

www.hollywoodsign.org, N. Highland Ave and Hollywood Blvd.
Los Angeles, CA 90028 (the view is always open).

No landmark or sign screams southern California, L.A., show business, or Hollywood like the Hollywood sign. If you are interested in getting a great view of the sign, head over to the intersection of N Highland Ave and Hollywood Boulevard. Here you will find the Hollywood and Highland Center. Designers of the center made it a point to make the distant sign the centerpiece of their structural composition and as such photo opportunities are plentiful throughout the facility.

 # COLE'S P.E. BUFFET
LOS ANGELES, CA

118 E. 6th St.
Los Angeles, CA 90014
(213) 622-4090
http://www.colesfrenchdip.com
http://youtu.be/UhSgAC_HhCg

Food: Yes
Live Music: No
Bar Hours: Sunday—Wednesday 11:30am-12:00am,
Thursday—Saturday 11:00am-2:00am
Type of Bar: Café
What to Drink: Red Car Named Desire
Why You Should Go: Real, genuine Los Angeles history
(not a lot of that around anymore), superb craft cocktails,
and the tasty French dip.

Established in 1908 on the ground floor of the Pacific Electric Red Car's primary hub, Cole's P.E. Buffet is a testament to an era, a shrine to the importance of the pub to the hardworking men and women of the country, and a symbol to a select number of dedicated bar owners devoted to the preservation of some of the greatest historical establishments across the nation.

THE HISTORY

Cole's P.E. Buffet owes its start to the Pacific Electric Railway, also known as the Red Car. The Red Car was a mass transit system in Southern California that used streetcars, light-rail, and buses interconnected throughout cities in Los Angeles and Orange County. At the center of the Red Car was their main depot, the Pacific Electric Building, which was located at 6th and Main Streets in downtown L.A. The depot became L.A.'s version of New York's Grand Central Station and it's here that Los Angeles' oldest, still-operating restaurant and saloon was started.

Founded by Henry Cole in 1908 on the ground floor of the Pacific Electric Building, Cole's was built to serve the 100,000-plus residents that passed through every day. Henry was an innovator, initially using varnished doors of retired Red Cars as table tops, and shortly after opening started L.A.'s first check cashing service from the bar. The check cashing business was so successful that in 1936, records show they cashed 176,000 checks for a value of $7,150,000.

The establishment quickly became a cornerstone of the Pacific Electric Railway's main terminal, and vastly popular among hardworking men and women of the area. Of course it probably didn't hurt that customers could grab a meal, a drink, and cash their payday checks all at a location conveniently situated on the way to and from work.

Cole's operated continuously for decades, but as the interstate road system was built in the 1950s and 1960s, the Red Cars eventually disappeared. The last train ran in 1961, after over a half-century of service.

With the closing of the Red Car service and, eventually, the hub upstairs, Cole's P.E. Buffet lost much of its clientele. To make matters worse, many businesses relocated out of downtown L.A., and the area fell into decline and seediness. By the 1980s and 1990s, the oldest bar in the city was teetering on the brink of closing, flirting with the titles of "dive" or "dump" and quickly gaining a bad reputation.

TODAY

Luckily in 2008 Cole's was purchased by 213 Nightlife, a company led by Los Angeles' own nightlife king and visionary, Cedd Moses. Cedd and 213 are considered proprietors of historic downtown L.A. bars and purchased the thread-worn saloon intending to both preserve it and return it to its previous glory.

After a year of renovations, Cole's re-opened in December of 2008 bringing back the traditional feel and look of the place from 1908. The décor and pictures look to have come from all corners and periods of Southern California's history and if you look through the peep holes in the hall leading to the bathrooms you can even spy a scene dating back to the early 1900s.

THE FOOD

Though its location and claim of the oldest restaurant and bar in the city of Los Angeles give it clout among some of the most historical places across the nation, it is Cole's greatest gift to the nation (invention of the French Dip Sandwich) that it is most known for today.

Though it is an ongoing debate with Philippe's (who also opened in 1908 and claims to be the inventor of the French Dip) Cole's claims that Henry Cole first dipped a roast beef sandwich into the drippings at the request of a customer with

recent dental work. The customer stated the French bread was too hard to eat without causing discomfort and requested it be dipped in juice to soften it. Henry, always willing to please his clientele, was happy to oblige and dipped the sandwich. It was an immediate hit as other customers saw what Henry had done and requested he do the same for them. And so from a man with recent dental work, some hard French bread, the caring heart of a bar owner, and the hungry eyes of his patrons, the French Dip was born.

So what is Cole's P.E. Buffet's French Dip like? Amazing, to put it simply. The beef itself is outstanding, but throw in some horseradish sauce, au jus, and an atomic pickle on the side and you have the must-try plate at Cole's . . . maybe even in all of downtown L.A.

THE DRINKS

Cole's has taken a spare-no-detail traditional approach to their cocktails and it shows with one of their most popular drinks, "The Red Car Named Desire!" The Red Car was created by one of Cole's bar managers and is a twist on the historic Manhattan containing a couple of the traditional ingredients and a few nontraditional ones like Cynar (an Italian bitter liqueur) and Luxardo Cherry Liqueur.

Watching the bartender make the drink is like watching one of the great artists paint, with no attention to detail spared. The drink is a pleasure to the senses, visually striking, aromatic and a great mixture of flavor. It is the must-try drink at Cole's.

http://youtu.be/Bqaz8MsNSbA

NEARBY DISTRACTIONS

Staples Center

www.staplescenter.com, 1111 S. Figueroa Street Los Angeles, CA 90015 (213) 742-7100 (operating hours vary by event, no tour offered).

At just 1.6 miles from Cole's, the Staples Center is literally just right down the road. Often considered the sports and entertainment center of the world, it hosts a very long list of sporting and entertainment events. Have a free night in L.A.? Check out the Staples Center, it's almost guaranteed to have something going on.

Santa Anita

www.santaanita.com, 285 West Huntington Drive Arcadia, CA 91007 (626) 574-7223 (simulcasting goes on year-round, live racing runs September-November).

Twenty miles and what seems like a world away from downtown L.A. and Cole's is horse racing's Santa Anita Park. Traditionally associated with the film and television industry (legends like Bing Crosby and Shirley Temple were known to be regulars) it's probably best known for hosting one of the greatest race horses in America's history: Seabiscuit. The track is open to tours every Saturday and Sunday of live racing season. The tour offers a rare behind-the-scenes glimpse into this storied track and the sport of horse racing.

OTHER NOTABLE AREA BARS

Ercoles Bar
1101 Manhattan Avenue Manhattan Beach, CA 90266 (310) 372-1997 (Monday-Sunday 10am-2am).

Since 1927 this Manhattan Beach gem has been a study in modesty. Not one ounce of pretense is to be found in this classic dive bar. They have basic beer on tap—Coors included—and some really great drink specials for some really great classic wells, like whiskies and gin. The food is dive-bar-basic: hot dogs and burgers and the like. The crowd is diverse and pleasant, and like the bar, humble and authentic.

Barney's Beanery
8447 Santa Monica Boulevard West Hollywood, CA (323) 654-2287 (Monday-Friday 10am-2am, Saturday-Sunday 9am-2am).

Opened at this location in 1927, Barney's is a beloved sports bar that's been serving the city continuously since it opened its doors. It's been in a slew of movies and has had a cast of notables and celebrities through its doors. On one particular night Jim Morrison, three sheets to the wind, pulled down his pants and took a leak right on the bar. He was immediately booted out of course, but a plaque honoring the event is clearly in place. Take a picture next to it for the album!

The Roost

**3100 Los Feliz Boulevard, Los Angeles, CA 90039 (323) 664-7272
(Monday-Sunday 12pm-2am).**

This Hollywood dive is known for two things: cheap drinks and popcorn. It's been around since the 1960s and from the looks of the décor it hasn't changed much in that time (the interior has been said to resemble the inside of grandma's house). It attracts a fairly diverse crowd composed of hipsters and old local regulars.

Formosa Café

**7156 Santa Monica Boulevard, West Hollywood, CA 90046 (323)
850-9050 (Monday-Friday 4pm-2am).**

Opened in 1925 this small café is a Hollywood landmark (seriously, it was declared a landmark in the 1990s). It's located directly adjacent to one of the most famous studio lots in the city—now Samuel Goldwyn Studio. Movies have been filmed there since the early 1920s and are still filmed there today. Because of its location, it's been a frequent watering hole for dozens of celebrities over the past century, from Humphrey Bogart to Brad Pitt.

SAN FRANCISCO AREA

The history of San Francisco is one of wickedness and debauchery. What a wonderful city to end this guide in! It didn't start out that way of course. In fact, San Francisco was little more than a Spanish mission and fort until 1849. After gold was discovered, the population boomed and smart entrepreneurs from around the world rushed to the Bay Area to make their fortunes—whether it be from mining or something else.

Because of the sheer amount of wealth—in the form of gold—that travelled through San Francisco, anything could be had. In one account of a standard mercantile store was a list of 110 different alcoholic beverages for sale, including Scotch ale, English porter, port, champagne, burgundy, claret, rum, gin and whiskey. There was, in short, no shortage of booze.

And places to consume booze were even more bountiful. The Barbary Coast, a three-block-long area of the most depraved booze joints in the country, drew thousands of gamblers, sailors, prostitutes and bandits every week. Here any kind of drink, drug or vice could be had for little, and human lives were worth even less.

In 1906 much of the area was leveled in the great earthquake and then subsequent fire. Most every bar—heck most every structure—was destroyed. Some remained standing, but most were rebuilt. The outcome is that any historic saloon in this area is a survivor and has a great story waiting to be discovered.

TRANSPORTATION: Yellow Cab Cooperative (In San Francisco) (415) 333-3333 (Monday-Sunday 24hrs). Luxor Cab Company (In San Francisco and Oakland) (415) 282-4141 (Monday-Sunday 24hrs).

ELIXIR SALOON

SAN FRANCISCO, CA

3200 16th Street
San Francisco, CA 94103
(415) 552-1633
http://www.elixirsf.com
http://youtu.be/ANwtfxrgsl8

Food: No
Live Music: No
Hours: Monday—Friday, 3pm-2am, Saturday 12pm-2am, Sunday 11am-2am
Type of Bar: Saloon
What to Drink: The Bloody Elixir
Why You Should Go: An original from the days of the Barbary Coast where human life was less important than the next drink.

Restored to its former glory in 2003 the Elixir has been in operation since 1858, making it one of the oldest continually running saloons in San Francisco. Today it is one of the top-rated bars in the country and home of the Build Your Own Bloody Mary as well as some of the best craft beers and cocktails in the area.

THE HISTORY

Located on the corner of 16th and Guerrero and smack dab in the middle of the area once known as the Barbary Coast, an area known for its bars and prostitutes, sits the Elixir Saloon. Originally opened in 1858, it is one of the oldest continually operating establishments on the West Coast and the second oldest in San Francisco still open today. To give you an idea of what the city was like when the saloon was open, simply consider that in 1851 San Francisco had 537 places serving alcohol and only 8 churches. Or, for every church there were 67 bars.

The first recorded owner was Hugh Mooney, who owned the bar from 1873 until 1893. In 1893, Mooney sold the bar to Patrick J. McGinnis Esquire, a prominent city lawyer. McGinnis owned it through the infamous earthquake of 1906—the cause of widespread fires that swept through the city and claimed thousands of structures including the Elixir. McGinnis immediately rebuilt his beloved bar in 1906/1907 (his original floor plan is still displayed proudly by the front door) making it the only bar in San Francisco to be rebuilt in the same location and by the same owner after the 1906 earthquake.

Also of note, during McGinnis' ownership was the period of Prohibition during which the Saloon was listed as a "Soft Drink Parlor." During this period there is no concrete evidence of it being turned into a speakeasy or of any illegal activity occurring at the site. But the current owner believes, and we agree, that a place like the Elixir didn't simply shut down or suspend all activity in regards to alcohol; few places ever truly did at the time. Instead McGinnis, as a well-informed lawyer, probably continued to operate the bar using his legal smarts to avoid any issues with the law.

As time progressed the bar changed owners, layouts, and even its name a few times. It was known as The Hunt-In Club from 1940-1965, which was the first known name change. From 1965-1985 it was Swede's, named after the owner and discussed in the book "The Great and Notorious Saloons of San Francisco." 1985-1990 saw the place transformed into a club known by two names, Club Corona and La Bandita, and was a popular gay and transvestite Latino bar. In 1990, it was Jack's Elixir Bar. And finally in 2003, "H"—the current owner— bought it, restored it and gave it the name it continues to be known by today.

Over the years the bar has changed, the clientele has changed and the neighborhood surrounding it has reinvented itself a time or two. But one thing that has never changed is the fact that the place has always been a bar (or a "Soft Drink Parlor"). Through the earthquakes, fires, worldwide tragedies and the push and pull of mainstream culture, the Elixir has remained a saloon. It is a true neighborhood bar that is ingrained into the

neighborhood, gives back part of what is given and is a place where anyone and everyone is welcome.

TODAY

Today the bar is owned by H. Joseph Ehrmann ("H") who, wanting to preserve the bar and its history, jumped at the chance to begin restoring it immediately after signing the papers. He told us the bar itself was hidden behind peeling paint and bumper stickers, the floor was more of a trampoline than a floor, the bathrooms were something we probably didn't want to know about and the ceiling was barely staying up. To put it simply, it was neglected and run down. H spent the next several months working, calling in favors from his friends and acquaintances, stripping the place down to its core and then returning it to its past luster.

In addition to the physical and visual improvements, H made some improvements to the Elixir's cocktail list. Though the traditional cocktail menu is intact, he added both seasonal and regional selections. From great local craft beers (some brewed specifically for the Elixir), cocktails that change with the season, and right down to H's specialty (The Bloody Elixir,) the place has a drink for everyone.

THE DRINKS

Often we list a drink that is a must-try, and we plan to do so here, but never have we listed one that has been more recognized than the Bloody Elixir—H's take on the Bloody Mary.

This drink made it to number four on GQ magazine's "20 Best Cocktails in America" for 2008, as well as local Audience Choice awards for 2005 and 2006, and the 2008 Editor's

Choice Best of Citysearch, San Francisco: Best Bloody Mary. Needless to say, if you find yourself in the Elixir it is at the top of the list of must-tries.

Every Saturday and Sunday morning, the Elixir also offers a Make Your Own Bloody Mary bar. Adding a piece or two of bacon makes for a unique and great tasting twist to the traditional drink.

NEARBY DISTRACTIONS

Fisherman's Wharf
www.fishermanswharf.org

Less than four miles from the Elixir is San Francisco's most popular tourist destination: Fisherman's Wharf. The Wharf features a long list of restaurants (some featuring breathtaking views of the bay and the Golden Gate Bridge), seafood stands (featuring outstanding clam chowder and Dungeness crab), hotels, street vendors, street performers, gift shops, an aquarium and even a few bars. Though it is almost always crowded with tourists, it's a must-visit location when in the area.

Trattoria Pinocchio
www.trattoriapinocchio.com, 401 Columbus Avenue, San Francisco, CA 94133 (415) 392-1472 (open for lunch and dinner 7 days a week).

Trattoria Pinocchio is less than three miles from the Elixir and worth every mile walked or driven. Owned by Sicily native and renowned Chef Giovanni Zocca, it has the best Italian food we've ever tasted. Featuring homemade pastas, pizzas, seafood and steaks it is a truly Italian dining experience and one not to be forgotten. So if you find yourself in the mood for Italian, look no further than Pinocchio's as you will not be disappointed.

HEINOLD'S FIRST AND LAST CHANCE

OAKLAND, CA

48 Webster Street in Jack London Square
Oakland CA 94607
510-839-6761
http://www.firstandlastchance.com
http://youtu.be/mSxoE2bM1tEType of Bar: Saloon

Food: No
Live Music: No
Hours: Monday 3pm-11pm, Tuesday—Thursday, Sunday
12pm-11pm, Friday—Saturday 12pm-1am
Type of Bar: Saloon
What to Drink: Local craft beer or glass of local wine
Why You Should Go: Connection to Jack London, last
surviving example of Gold Rush-era saloon.

Here is a piece of history that few know: Jack London, one of the most famous and prolific writers in the world, owed his career—some even say his life—to this small bar in Oakland, California.

THE HISTORY

Originally built on a dock in Oakland's East Bay in 1880, Heinold's Saloon was constructed from the timbers of an old whaling ship and used as a bunkhouse for men working at the nearby oyster beds. Johnny Heinhold bought the place in 1883 for $100 and, with the help of a ship's carpenter, transformed the place into a saloon specifically built for the seafaring men roaming the waterfront.

After operating successfully for over 30 years, the bar was renamed Heinhold's First and Last Chance Saloon for two notable reasons. First, during the 1920s the city of Alameda was dry and Heinhold's just happened to be right next to the dock for the ferry running between Oakland and Alameda. It was literally the commuters' first and last chance for a drink on their way to and from Alameda.

Second, the bar also served as the first and last chance for a drink for servicemen deploying and returning home from the Port of Oakland. To have a drink here is a fairly powerful tradition as is evidenced by the memorabilia strewn throughout the bar today.

Over the years, the saloon has played host to millions of patrons

from all walks of life. It was a huge part of legendary writer Jack London's life beginning when he was only 10 years old.

The bar served as the source of ideas for many of his books as he listened to the tales of visitors from all over the world. It was in this saloon that Jack met Alexander McLean who was the inspiration for the powerful and morally questionable Captain Wolf Larsen in the novel, "The Sea Wolf". McLean was known to shanghai drunks in the saloon and force them into service on his ship nicknamed, "The Hell Ship" because of his rumored cruelty at sea (he was probably more in line with the fictitious captain of the Sea-Wolf than anyone ever imagined).

On Wednesday, April 18th, 1906 an estimated 7.9 magnitude earthquake struck Northern California's Bay Area causing wide-spread devastation. The resulting fire destroyed a large percentage of what wasn't destroyed by the earthquake and the total death toll in San Francisco is estimated to have been at least 3,000 people. Ironically, The First and Last Chance was one of the few structures in the entire Bay Area left standing, though it had some additional dimensions added.

The earthquake caused the pilings under the saloon to settle into the mud, some more than others, giving the saloon a noticeable slope from the front to the back of the bar.

Unsuccessful efforts were made to shore up and level the floor and as such, the slope continues even today. When you step in, you also step down and immediately notice that everything in the bar is sloped, even the bar itself. The sloping isn't quite enough to make your drinks slide down the bar, though you do tend to keep a firm grasp on them just in case. The bartenders are accustomed to putting just the right amount in your glasses to avoid accidental spillage. We did a little experimenting and found that after a few drinks, things tend to level out.

TODAY

This place is more akin to a museum than a bar, and most of the items inside should probably actually be in a museum. You can literally walk in, order a drink and sit down at the same table where Jack London used to study, write, and listen to tales from the ever-present adventurers and sailors.

The artifacts on the wall are all historic and protected by a simple layer of chicken wire. Take a close look at the clock on the wall, it doesn't move and hasn't since the earthquake of

1906 (there was nothing wrong with it, Heinold simply never restarted it). From the stained ceiling caused by the gas lamps (still in operation), to the antiques on the ceiling and walls, right down to the very floor, this place really tells the history of San Francisco and Oakland.

A few modern touches have changed its exterior just a bit. For example the place is no longer sitting on the dock (the city extended the landmass to encompass the bar and other surroundings), there is now a patio, and a 1/2 size replica of Jack London's cabin built from the very timbers of his original Alaskan cabin (there's also an identical cabin made from the remaining timbers located in Alaska as well). But with the exception of the surrounding landmass, a modern bathroom and a few other updates to make the place safe, it is as close to original as you could possibly hope for.

Speaking of the bathroom. If you happen to find yourself at the First and Last Chance and are with a first timer or someone not as educated as you've become from reading this book, then you have the perfect victim for a great joke.

If anyone in your party happens to go to the bathroom ask the bartender to say hello to them via the hidden speaker. Throw the bartender a couple of bucks, give them the individual's name, and watch as they really make the visit memorable.

THE DRINKS

There's a full-service bar at the First and Last Chance Saloon, so order up whatever you might like. Of particular interest are the local craft beers on tap and the local wines (we had a great

conversation with their wine distributor and he assured us this was local stuff).

But it somehow seems more fitting to simply sip something on the rocks. That's what Jack MacLean probably would've had as he sat in the corner eyeing the drunks and trying to figure out which one to kidnap.

A whiskey over ice is a drink worthy of drinking at Heinold's.

NEARBY DISTRACTIONS

Jack London Square

www.jacklondonsquare.com, 466 Water St. Oakland, CA 94607 (510) 645-9292 (open year round but business times vary).

Heinold's First and Last Chance Saloon sits right in the middle of Oakland's renowned Jack London Square. Named after the very man whose life was forever changed by the storied First and Last Chance Saloon, Jack London Square is steeped in maritime lore. Lining the natural estuary leading to the San Francisco Bay, the square contains a long list of restaurants, shops, businesses, walking paths and, of course, marinas. Events like live music, fundraisers and farmers market are common so be sure to check the events schedule posted on their website before heading out.

USS Hornet Museum

www.uss-hornet.org, 707 West Hornet Avenue Alameda, CA 94501 (510) 521-8448 (Monday-Sunday 1pm-5pm).

Keeping in the maritime tradition and in the spirit of Heinold's

First and Last Chance Saloon, a visit to the USS Hornet is a fitting destination. Less than four miles from Heinold's, the USS Hornet is a decorated World War 2-era aircraft carrier that participated in the Doolittle Raid, saw action in Vietnam and participated in some of the first moon missions.

OTHER NOTABLE AREA BARS

Saloon
1232 Grant Avenue San Francisco, CA (415) 989-7666 (Monday-Friday 12pm-2am).

This North Beach watering hole was founded in 1861, so it's a true remnant of the city's wilder days. The structure survived the 1906 earthquake and fire (it's said the fire brigades kept the fire away to protect the hookers upstairs) so when you drink here you're drinking in the real deal. It is maybe one of the scariest places you'll ever set foot into. The bouncers look like rejects from a biker gang and the décor is full of dive bar clichés, but it really is a great place. They have live music and some of the best blues bands in the Bay play here.

Little Shamrock
807 Lincoln Way San Francisco CA (415) 661-0060 (Monday-Thursday 3pm-2am, Friday 2pm-2am, Saturday-Sunday 1pm-2am).

Opened sometime in the early 1890s (the claim is 1893 but there are several problems with that claim), the Little Shamrock rocks its status as second oldest bar in San Francisco differently than the oldest (the Saloon). Chiefly, it doesn't stink as badly. After a century it can't help but have a bit of a stench, but the bathrooms are clean and the service is friendly. It's become a favorite locals' bar and has earned a good reputation over the years.

The Buena Vista
2765 Hyde St. San Francisco, CA 94109 (415) 474-5044
(Monday-Friday 9am-2am, Saturday-Sunday 8am-2am).

If you find yourself in need of a warming cup of coffee while visiting the area, why not make it Irish and head on over to the Buena Vista? Featuring a legendary cup of Irish Coffee developed back in 1952 when owner Jack Koeppler challenged Stanton Delaplane, to help re-create the legendary Irish Coffee served at Shannon Airport in Ireland. After much research (that is, repetitive mixing and drinking) and a trip back to Ireland, they were able to create the delicious recipe still served today. Located next to the Powell-Hyde Cable Car's last stop and close to Fisherman's Wharf, it is a favorite among tourists and locals alike.

INDEX

BUCKET LIST

Check these bars off your bucket list, and get ready to add more!

- ☐ Billy Goat Tavern
- ☐ Bridge Cafe
- ☐ Buckhorn Exchange
- ☐ Chope's Bar
- ☐ City Tavern
- ☐ Cole's P.E. Buffet
- ☐ Crystal Palace
- ☐ Ear Inn
- ☐ El Chapultepec
- ☐ El Patio
- ☐ Elixir Saloon
- ☐ Esquire Tavern
- ☐ Fraunces Tavern
- ☐ Frolic Room
- ☐ Green Door Tavern
- ☐ Green Mill
- ☐ Hala Kahiki
- ☐ Heinold's First and Last Chance

- [ ] Kon Tiki
- [ ] La Posta
- [ ] McGillin's Olde Ale House
- [ ] McSorley's Old Ale House
- [ ] Menger Bar
- [ ] Mother's Original
- [ ] My Brother's Bar
- [ ] Old '76 House
- [ ] Old Town Bar
- [ ] Palacio Bar
- [ ] Pioneer Saloon
- [ ] Rosa's Cantina
- [ ] Scholz Garten
- [ ] Scoot Inn
- [ ] Simon's Tavern
- [ ] Tap Room at the Hotel Congress
- [ ] The Buffet
- [ ] The Tavern
- [ ] Tonga Hut
- [ ] Townhouse (Del Monte Speakeasy)
- [ ] Warren Tavern
- [ ] White Horse Tavern

CONNECT WITH US!

Questions or comments about the bars in here? Are we completely, arrogantly wrong about the details? Do YOU have a Bucket List Bar™ we just have to include in the next book? Let us know!

Mail
Bucket List Bars
c/o AO Media LLC
2015 Cotton Ave.
Las Cruces, NM 88001

Email
info@bucketlistbars.com

Find Us on the Web
http://www.bucketlistbars.com
http://www.drunkenhistory.com

Follow Us on Twitter
@BucketListBars
@DrunkenHistory

Connect on Facebook
Facebook.com/drunkenhistory

ABOUT THE AUTHORS

Dr. Clint Lanier

Fascinated by the hidden history of bars, Clint Lanier has traveled the world to find out-of-the-way watering holes with great stories to tell. From the juke joints of the Mississippi Delta, to the cantinas of Mexico, he's always on the lookout for the next saloon, tavern, or dive that brings a neighborhood or a whole city together. When not on the road, he is an assistant professor at New Mexico State University in Las Cruces, New Mexico.

Derek Hembree

As a military brat, Derek Hembree began traveling and exploring the world at a very young age. A bartender during his college years and an adventurer at heart, he is intrigued by historic bars, their stories, the art of mixology, and sharing it all with the world. Along with traveling and bars, Derek is passionate about finding the perfect wave, the freshest powder, wakesurfing and exploring the world on two wheels.